FOUR POINT
Listening and Speaking 2
ENGLISH FOR ACADEMIC PURPOSES

Second Edition

FOUR POINT
Listening and Speaking 2
ENGLISH FOR ACADEMIC PURPOSES

Second Edition

BETSY PARRISH

Hamline University

Series Editor: KEITH S. FOLSE

Ann Arbor
University of Michigan Press

ISBN: 978-0-472-03742-1

2021   2020   2019   2018   4   3   2   1

Acknowledgments

Thanks to Anne DeMuth from Hamline University for her valuable feedback on the lecture on language acquisition in Unit 1. Thanks to Fahima Aziz from the School of Business at Hamline University for sharing data from her studies on the lives of women in Bangladesh who have been recipients of micro-credit, which led to the development of some activities in Unit 3. Thanks to students at the Minnesota English Language Program, particularly those in Arlys Arnold's class, for contributing their ideas on effective presentations in their cultures in Unit 1.

I am grateful for all the valuable feedback I received along the way from: my editor, Kelly Sippell; the developmental editor, Robyn Brinks Lockwood; our series editor, Keith Folse; and my fellow team member, Larry Zwier.

Finally, thanks to my family for their unending patience and support.

The publisher, series editor, and author would like to thank the educational professionals whose reviews helped shape the *Four Point* series, particularly those from these institutions:

> Auburn University
> Boston University CELOP
> Central Piedmont Community College
> Colorado State University
> Daytona Beach Community College
> Duke University
> Durham Technical College
> Georgia State University
> Harding University
> Hillsborough Community College
> Northern Virginia Community College, Alexandria Campus
> Oregon State University
> University of California, San Diego
> University of Nevada at Las Vegas
> University of North Carolina, Charlotte
> Valencia Community College

The University of Michigan Press would like to thank these individuals for their involvement and support on this project:

> Voice talent: Kelsey Dean, Pat Grimes, Scott Ham, Sheryl Leicher, Shaun Manning, Karen Pitton, and Laurel Stroud.

Acting talent: Wai Lee Chan, Jake Christensen, Alex Dean, Kelsey Dean, Angie Feak, Chris Feak, Scott Ham, Nathan Mosseri, Sun Hyun Park, and Morgan Peterson.

For filming and production of the video and audio: Elie Mosseri of Mosseri Enterprises with Fred Goryzk (video) and Doug Trevethan (audio).

Grateful acknowledgment is made to the following authors, publishers, and individuals for permission to reprint copyrighted or previously published materials.

Jennifer Campbell for permission to use the text of her Three Minute Thesis presentation "Nanocantilevers and Medical Diagnostics" (Queens University School of Graduate Studies), April 2012.

Kathleen Herber for slides used in Unit 3.

Morgan & Claypool Publishers for excerpt from *Engineering and Sustainable Community Development* by Juan Lucena, Jen Schneider, and Jon A. Leydens, copyright © 2010.

Ozpolitic.com for 'Bullseye' and 'Mickey Mouse' model from http://www.ozpolitic.com/articles/environment-society-economy.html.

Random House for excerpts from *The Great Inflation and Its Aftermath* by Robert Samuelson, Copyright © 2010.

University of Michigan English Language Institute for transcript excerpts STP355MG011, LEL215S6150, LEPROFESSOR65JG121 from the Michigan Corpus of Academic Spoken English (MICASE) micase.elicorpora.info. "The Parthenon Frieze" and "Autism and Vaccines" and from the Michigan Corpus of Upper-level Student Papers (MICUSP) micusp.elicorpora.info.

University of Michigan Press for "Language and Dialect" from *Understanding Language Structure, Interaction, and Variation, Third Edition,* by Steven Brown, Salvatore Attardo, and Cynthia Vigliotti, Copyright © 2014; "The Power of Waves" from *Category 5: The Story of Camille* by J.A. Howard, Copyright © 2005.

Every effort has been made to contact the copyright holders for permission to reprint borrowed material. We regret any oversights that may have occurred and will rectify them in future printings of this book.

Contents

1 Applied Linguistics: Learning a Language   1

Part 1: Benefits of Bilingualism   1

Effective Presentations   2

Strategy: Listening for/Including the Key Components of a Presentation   3

Speaking: Focusing the Audience on Important Information   5

Listening 1: Student Presentation: Listening for the Key Components of a Presentation   8

Making an Impromptu Speech   9

Part 2: Language and Dialects   9

Reading: Language and Dialect   10

Strategy: Recognizing (Listening for) and Giving Definitions   14

Speaking: Giving Examples and Explanations   17

Listening 2: Visiting a Professor during Office Hours   19

Part 3: Learning a First or Second Language   21

Speaking: Intonation with Tag Questions and Rhetorical Questions   21

Research Strategy: Taking Good Notes   23

Vocabulary Power   26

Listening 3: Lecture: The Nature of First and Second Language Acquisition   27

Oral Arguments   28

Rapid Vocabulary Review   29

Synthesizing: Projects and Presentations   30

Vocabulary Log   31

2 Geology: Natural Disasters   33

Part 1: Wildfires   33

Strategy: Listening for and Describing Processes, Developments, and Changes   34

Speaking: Clarifying   37

Listening 1: Student Presentation: Listening for Processes, Developments, and Changes   39

Making an Impromptu Speech   39

Part 2: The Nature of Waves   **40**
   Reading: The Power of Waves   40
   Strategy: Activating and Using Prior Knowledge   44
   Speaking: Discussing New Concepts   45
   Listening 2: Handling Informal Classroom Interactions   47

Part 3: What Is a Tsunami?   **50**
   Strategy: Listening to a Lecture with Visual Aids   51
   Research Strategy: Determining the Validity of Sources   53
   Vocabulary Power   54
   Listening 3: Lecture: What Causes Tsunamis?   55
   Group Project   56
   Rapid Vocabulary Review   57
   Synthesizing: Projects and Presentations   58
   Vocabulary Log   59

3 Economics: Inflation and Microeconomics   **61**

Part 1: Inflation   **61**
   Strategy: Listening for and Discussing Problems and Solutions   62
   Speaking: Hedging   65
   Listening 1: Student Presentation: Listening for Problems and Solutions   67
   Making an Impromptu Speech   71

Part 2: Exploring Economic Issues   **72**
   Reading: Inflation Refashioned   73
   Strategy: What to Do When You Don't Understand   77
   Speaking: Boosting   78
   Listening 2: Assigning Tasks on a Group Project   80

Part 3: Women and Microfinancing   **82**
   Strategy: Connecting Lectures to Readings or Previously   83
     Learned Material
   Research Strategy: Using the REAP Method   85
   Vocabulary Power   87
   Listening 3: Lecture: Is Microfinancing the Solution?   88
   Oral Arguments   89
   Rapid Vocabulary Review   90
   Synthesizing: Projects and Presentations   91
   Vocabulary Log   92

4 History: Ancient Civilizations   94

Part 1: Classical Civilizations   94
Strategy: Listening for and Providing Supporting Details and Evidence   95
Speaking: Providing a Chronology   97
Listening 1: Student Presentation: Listening for Supporting Details   100
    and Evidence
Making an Impromptu Speech   100

Part 2: Monuments in Culture   101
Reading: The Parthenon Frieze   102
Strategy: Listening for and Identifying Others' Opinions   106
Speaking: Leading a Group Discussion and Holding the Floor   107
Listening 2: Leading a Group Discussion and Holding the Floor   110

Part 3: The Emergence of the Roman Empire   112
Strategy: Listening to Lecture Introductions   113
Research Strategy: Types of Sources   115
Vocabulary Power   116
Listening 3: Lecture: Augustus and the Roman Empire   117
Panel Discussion   118
Rapid Vocabulary Review   119
Synthesizing: Projects and Presentations   120
Vocabulary Log   121

5 Health Sciences: Neurological Disorders   123

Part 1: Strokes   123
Strategy: Listening for and Talking about Statistics and Trends   124
Speaking: Presenting Proposals   127
Listening 1: Student Presentation: Listening for Statistics and   128
    General Information
Making an Impromptu Speech   128

Part 2: Autism across the World   129
Reading: Autism and Vaccines: Where Does the Evidence Stand?   130
Strategy: Listening for and Making Educated Guesses   135
Speaking: Presenting an Argument or Drawing Attention to a   137
    Strong Belief
Listening 2: Recognizing Strong Beliefs and Points of View   139

Part 3: Causes of Communication Difficulties   **141**

Strategy: Managing Open Lecture Style   141

Research Strategy: Primary Research in Depth   146

Vocabulary Power   147

Listening 3: Lecrture: Aphasia and Assistive Technology and   148
    Communication

Panel Discussion   148

Rapid Vocabulary Review   150

Synthesizing: Projects and Presentations   151

Vocabulary Log   152

6 Engineering: Management Science   **154**

Part 1: Problem Solving   **154**

Strategy: Listening to Short Pitches (or Elevator Speeches)   155

Speaking: Being Compelling and Persuasive   157

Listening 1: Student Presentation: Listening to a 3MT™   158

Making an Impromptu Speech   159

Part 2: Sustainability   **159**

Reading: Engineers and Sustainable Development (1980s to   160
    the Present)

Strategy: Listening for and Making Objections (Refuting)   168

Speaking: Managing a Q & A Session   171

Listening 2: Managing a Q & A Session   172

Part 3: Engineering Innovation   **175**

Strategy: Listening for Ideal Breaks for Interruptions   175

Research Strategy: Creating an Outline   178

Vocabulary Power   180

Listening 3: Lecture: Engineering Innovations: Tunnels   181

Group Presentation   182

Rapid Vocabulary Review   183

Synthesizing: Projects and Presentations   184

Vocabulary Log   185

Appendix 1: Review of Note-Taking Formats   187

Appendix 2: Debate (Oral Arguments) Guidelines   191

Series Overview

Four Point is a six-volume series designed for English language learners whose primary goal is to succeed in an academic setting. While grammar points and learning strategies are certainly important, academic English language learners (ELLs) need skills-based books that focus on the four primary skills of reading, writing, listening, and speaking in a realistic, integrated format, as well as the two primary language bases of vocabulary and grammar. To this end, the *Four Point* series offers a unique combination of instructional material and activities that truly require students to read, write, speak, and listen in a multitude of combinations.

Four Point has three English for Academic Purposes (EAP) levels. While academic listening and speaking skills are covered in one volume and academic reading and writing are covered in another, *all four skills are integrated throughout all books,* so a given task may focus on speaking and listening but have a reading and/or writing component to it as well.

Developing the Four Skills in *Four Point*

The series covers the four academic skills of reading, writing, listening, and speaking, while providing reinforcement and systematic recycling of key vocabulary issues and further exposure to grammar issues. The goal of this series is to help students improve their ability in each of these four critical skills and thereby enable the students to have sufficient English to succeed in their final academic setting, whether it be community college, college, or university as an undergraduate or graduate student.

Many ELLs report great difficulties upon entering their academic courses after they leave the safe haven of their English class with other nonnative speakers and their sympathetic and caring ESL teachers. Their academic instructors speak quickly, give long reading assignments due the next day, deliver classroom lectures and interactions at rapid, native speed, and sometimes balk at the excessive errors in their ELLs' writing. In sum, the ELL who has gone through a sheltered classroom setting is in for a rather rude awakening in a new learning situation where English is taken for granted and no one seems to understand or care much about the new reality of the dilemmas facing ELLs, a setting in which they are treated the same as LI students. Through these materials, we hope to lessen the shock of such an awakening.

The activities in *Four Point* achieve the goal of helping ELLs experience what life beyond the ESL classroom is like while they are still in a sheltered classroom. This chart explains some of the activities in *Four Point*:

Reading	Listening
Students will read longer, more difficult readings on interesting and challenging academic topics that better represent the array and level in a college classroom. Extensive pleasure reading is good, but ELLs need practice for the type of reading they will find in their academic course books as well. Strategies introduced in the books will help develop the skills necessary to succeed with academic material.	Students will have to listen to presentations, group discussions, and lectures to not only pick out details and facts but also practice identifying speaker opinions, recognizing definitions, and synthesizing lectures with other material. Students will also gain experience listening to multiple native speakers at the same time as they discuss academic work and topics in realistic settings.
Writing	**Speaking**
Students will write both short and long assignments that mirror authentic college assignments in addition to research papers. Special emphasis is given to the academic writing skills of paraphrasing, summarizing, and synthesizing.	Students will practice both short and long speaking activities and thereby develop their speaking fluency, an area often overlooked in many ESL books. Students will also practice leading a discussion, hedging and boosting, and managing Q & A.

Maximizing Coverage of the Two Primary Language Bases

ESL materials have come a long way from the old days of equating repetitive grammar drills for speaking practice or copying sentences for writing practice. However, in the ensuing shift from focus on language to focus on communication, very little was developed to address the needs of academic ELLs who need to do much more in English than engage in conversations about daily events, fill out job applications, or read short pieces of text for pleasure. It was the proverbial "baby being thrown out with the bath water" as emphasis on grammar and vocabulary was downplayed. However, in order to participate in academic settings, our ELLs certainly need focused activities to develop and then maintain their use of vocabulary and grammar. Toward this end, the *Four*

Point series provides further exposure of key grammar issues without overt practice activities.

More important, these books focus very heavily on vocabulary because ELLs realize that they are way behind their native-speaker counterparts when it comes to vocabulary. Each book highlights between 125–150 key vocabulary items, including individual words, compound words, phrasal verbs, short phrases, idioms, metaphors, collocations, and longer set lexical phrases. In learning vocabulary, the two most important features are frequency of retrievals (i.e., in exercises) and the spacing between these retrievals. Spaced rehearsal is accomplished in two ways. First, after words appear in the textbook, they will reappear multiple times afterward. Second, interactive web-based exercises provide more than ample opportunities for ELLs to practice their vocabulary learning through spaced rehearsals at the student's convenience (www.press.umich.edu/elt/compsite/4Point/).

General Overview of Units

Each of the books is divided into six units with numerous activities within each unit. The material in each of the volumes could be covered in ten to twelve weeks, but this number is flexible depending on the students and the teacher, and the depth to which the material is practiced.

Using the Activities in This Book

Each unit includes three listening passages within a field of academic study (i.e., one student presentation, one group discussion or interaction, and one lecture). The group discussions and interactions appear in the online video scenes. The exercises accompanying the passages are meant to strengthen a range of listening and speaking skills, notably:

- noticing main points
- understanding classroom discourse
- using academic language functions
- recognizing signal words and phrases
- developing vocabulary
- synthesizing information

In addition to a more general listening comprehension task, most units include a specific listening focus, such as managing open lecture style, using visual aids to take notes, and connecting lecture content to other material. The student presentations range in length from 4 to 7 minutes, and the lectures range in length from 11 to 17 minutes. The lectures are sold separately as MP3 files (audio download) (978-0-472-00362-4). The video scenes are available and can be found online at www.press.umich.edu/esl/compsite/4Point/.

Getting Started

A range of pre-listening discussion questions is included; each has the purpose of activating prior knowledge about, making predictions about, and generating interest in the topics in the unit. Often these questions provide opportunities for students to anticipate content and, therefore, may be revisited throughout the unit. All of the pre-listening questions lead to pair or small group discussions.

Research Strategies

Each unit introduces a research strategy, allowing students to develop a fundamental knowledge of concepts necessary to succeed in research at the college level. As students' experiences vary, it is important to supply them with this base. It is certainly possible that students can draw on content that works particularly well for them in their discipline or other classes as they practice and develop their skills throughout the text. Other types of strategies and skills—those related to listening, speaking, and vocabulary—are highlighted at various points. Listening strategies appear in a display box with a short explanation and/or signal words and tips. Speaking strategies include key words and phrases. All include practice activities.

Listening Activities

Each unit contains three listening passages: a presentation, a discussion, and a lecture. The passages are long and authentic in an effort to mirror realistic college experiences and prepare students for success. Listening passages feature false starts, digressions, and pauses. The listening passages allow students to practice the strategy and/or hear the signal words or phrases in use.

Vocabulary Activities

Vocabulary Power activities appear once in each unit. The words chosen for these tasks are ones that may appear in a variety of academic settings. These activities serve to further develop students' academic vocabulary base. These words are likely to be useful to the students as they move on to the synthesizing activities at the end of each unit as well as to the additional vocabulary activities: the Rapid Vocabulary Review, which focuses on synonyms and combinations and associations, and the Vocabulary Log. Students could also be asked to listen to portions of the lecture again to discover if they recognize the words used in context.

In-Class and Out-of-Class Interactions/Classroom Discourse

In addition to the lectures, each unit includes activities designed to prepare students for the in-class interactions they are likely to encounter in post-secondary classrooms. Throughout the units, students participate in group activities that allow them to use the speaking phrases taught in the unit. Other activities include oral arguments, panel presentations, and other types of in-depth discussions. Each unit contains an impromptu speech that allows the opportunity for students to practice speaking spontaneously about academic topics.

In addition, the audio includes several features of everyday language that are designed to help make the audio and video more realistic for students. Also, in the attempt to help students understand more than professional native speakers, the videos feature fluent non-native speakers in typical academic roles to provide models and to better replicate university settings.

The video scenes are provided on the companion website (www.press.umich.edu/elt/compsite/4Point/) to analyze for language, tone, and nonverbal cues as well as to generate discussion on academic listening and speaking tasks. Throughout the interaction, the students use some of the phrases and employ the strategies taught in the unit—and, in a few cases, do not use the best communication strategies. ELLs will have the opportunity to hear the phrases used in a natural conversation, practice their listening skills, analyze verbal and nonverbal communication skills of the speakers, and think critically about and discuss the interaction with their classmates. Questions in the book require students to listen for certain phrases and identify what they mean; to notice the tone of voice and think about how it changes the dynamics of a discussion; to recognize the influence of nonverbal communication by increasing their awareness of facial expressions, gestures, and other cues; and to compile all of these ideas into an analytical discussion about the interaction as a whole and what can be useful for students when they are in academic groups, especially with native speakers.

Reading Tasks

Each unit includes a reading generally used as the impetus for more extensive speaking and language activities and as a way to practice the strategies. As such, they do not include detailed comprehension questions. As the topics in the units are recent, the instructor could easily supplement a unit with current online readings.

Synthesizing: Projects and Presentations

The summative task for each unit includes four projects that mirror authentic assignments students are likely to encounter and encourage practice of the listening and speaking concepts. Students prepare projects and presentations based on what they have learned via the lectures, readings, discussions, or online or library research. For group projects, students should be given adequate time to clarify group roles and to work on their projects.

Rapid Vocabulary Review and Vocabulary Log

A vocabulary review task appears at the end of each unit and gives students another opportunity to check their understanding of key words and phrases. The correct answer is a synonym or brief definition. Crucial to the vocabulary acquisition process is the initial noticing of unknown vocabulary. ELLs must notice the vocabulary in some way, and this noticing then triggers awareness of the item and draws the learner's attention to the word in all subsequent encounters, whether the word is read in a passage or heard in a conversation or lecture. To facilitate noticing and then multiple retrievals of new vocabulary, we have included a chart listing 25 key vocabulary items at the end of each unit. This Vocabulary Log has three columns and requires students to provide a definition or translation in the second column and then an original example or note about usage in the third column. As demonstrated in *Vocabulary Myths* (Folse 2004, University of Michigan Press), there is no research showing that a definition is better than a translation or vice-versa, so we suggest that you let ELLs decide which one they prefer. After all, this log is each student's individual vocabulary notebook, so students should use whatever information is helpful to them and that will help them remember and use the vocabulary item. If the log information is not deemed useful, the learner will not review this material—which defeats the whole purpose of keeping the notebook. In the third column, students can use the word in a phrase or sentence, or they can also add usage information about the word such as *usually negative, very formal sounding,* or *used only with the word* launch.

Applied Linguistics: Learning a Language

How people acquire language—whether as a first or second (or third or fourth) language—is a major area of study in the field of Linguistics. Linguists have developed several theories about how languages are acquired, and these theories attempt to explore the way languages are retained, the factors that affect learning, and how languages are taught. This unit explores some of these theories and factors.

Part 1: Benefits of Bilingualism

Getting Started

When people move and live in a place with a different culture than their own, they often raise their children to be bilingual and often become bilingual themselves. It can be a challenge to maintain aspects of their original culture while also becoming part of their new culture. Answer these questions with a partner.

1. What are the benefits of knowing and being able to speak more than one language?

2. What are some of the challenges that bilinguals face?

Effective Presentations

Certain elements are expected in presentations given to a North American audience. Including these key components is one important part of making a good presentation. Use the chart to list some of the characteristics that make a presentation effective. Then compare lists with a partner.

What makes a presentation effective?	What makes a presentation ineffective?
Involve the audience	
Maintain good eye contact	
Speak loudly and clearly	

University students from around the world were asked what they think makes a presentation effective in North America. Decide whether you agree or disagree. Discuss with a partner.

Components of an Effective Presentation		
Student/Culture	Elements of an Effective Presentation	Agree or Disagree?
Ali from Saudi Arabia	Go straight to the main point	
Esther from Korea	Use visual aids; your audience won't remember your presentation if there are no visual aids	
Xianghong Liu from China	Involve the audience	
Sina from Iran	Start with a story, famous saying, or proverb	
Xianghong Liu from China	Use the standard language of the country, not a regional dialect	
Jose from Spain	Use many technical words, or specific terminology, to show that you know the topic very well	D
Jose from Spain	Don't speak about subtopics or points you are going to speak about in the introduction	
Tai from Vietnam	Summarize the whole presentation at the end	

Strategy: Listening for and Including the Key Components of a Presentation

In most academic disciplines, students must conduct studies and report their findings to peers, research groups, professors, or colleagues at workshops or conferences. Good speakers include key components and use certain phrases to make their presentation both academic and comprehensible.

Hook (thought-provoking questions and surprising statistics are common hooks)

> Have you ever wondered what it is like to be bilingual?
>
> Less than X percent of the world is bilingual.
>
> Last year, only X percent of the students in U.S. secondary schools studied a second language.

Purpose

> I was interested in . . . .
>
> The purpose of my study/research was . . . .
>
> In my study, I was looking at/researching . . . .
>
> I wanted to determine/see/learn/find out . . . .
>
> Today I'm reporting on my study of . . . .
>
> My goal was to solve the problem . . . .
>
> Another point of my research was . . . .

Results

> You will notice that more than X percent of the data . . . .
>
> A large number of subjects said . . . .
>
> Only X percent said . . . .
>
> My results show that . . . .
>
> These numbers conflict with earlier research.

Conclusions

> As you can see, my results prove . . . .
>
> My data allows me to say . . . .
>
> This offsets . . . .
>
> My conclusions are . . . .
>
> It would seem that . . . .
>
> From this it can be concluded that . . . .

*Note: Results and conclusions will be discussed in more depth throughout the text.

Practice Activity: Listening for/Including the Key Components of a Presentation

Work with a small group. Conduct a small study using your classmates as subjects. Investigate their experiences with language learning in general or find out about their experiences using English and their first language. Questions may include when they first started studying English, how many years they've studied, or how many years of English were required for them to graduate. Interview as many members of the class as possible in 20 minutes.

Topic:	
Questions	Results
Question 1 When did you start learning english	Born 5 yo , Elementary
Question 2 Is english hard, if so why do you keep on learning english.	No Hard, will be easy in the future Hard, they want to study in the US
Question 3 Point out the difference between english and your native language.	Everything Everything
Question 4 Are you confident when speaking to an American in english ?	Yes Not confident

Look at your results and then make some notes to use as the key components for a possible presentation: a hook, a purpose, some results, and some conclusions. Write a few lines for a presentation.

Hook _____

_____

Purpose _____

_____

Results _____

_____

Conclusions _____

_____

Speaking

Focusing the Audience on Important Information

In presentations, lectures, academic discussions, and even in general conversations, speakers need to draw attention to their main points. Native speakers are able to identify the main points because they are usually signaled with versions of certain phrases.

These are some of the questions I wanted to research.
[Basically], my research question is/was . . . .
The main point of my research is. . . .
What I'm stressing is . . . .
What you need to remember is . . . .
The important thing is . . . .
The primary reason is . . . .
Most importantly/Most important . . . .
A major [development] is . . . .
The [crucial] difference is . . . .
What is [critical, necessary, vital, paramount, significant, essential, mandatory] . . . .
So, what do these results tell us?
As you can see . . . .

Read the information about the Office of Educational Research and Improvement (OERI). Think about presenting this information as a formal presentation in an educational setting. Identify what you consider to be the most important information. Edit the text as needed to make sure the most important information is signaled. Then discuss your main points with a small group.

The Office of Educational Research and Improvement (OERI) provides national leadership in cultivating and expanding the public's fundamental knowledge and understanding of education. Moreover, OERI aggressively promotes the application of such knowledge to improve practice in the classroom. OERI also monitors the state of education and stimulates excellence and equity in education and the achievement of the National Education Goals by spurring reform in the school systems throughout the United States. OERI accomplishes these activities through its active collaboration with researchers, teachers, school administrators, librarians, parents, students, employers, and policy-makers.

OERI directs, coordinates, and recommends policy for activities that are designed to accomplish the following:

- Improve the quality of education and ensure access to equal educational opportunities for all individuals.

- Conduct basic and applied research on the teaching and learning process; the economic, social, and policy contexts of education; and other areas defined as high priority.

- Collect and analyze statistical data on the current condition of education and project education trends.

- Demonstrate, disseminate, and adapt new knowledge and practices to various education settings.

- Support learning opportunities through libraries, the information superhighway, and emerging technologies.

- Promote coordination between the Department's education research and development programs and the related activities of other federal agencies.

- Forge a national consensus with respect to a long-term agenda for education research, development, dissemination, and other activities through collaborative efforts with the National Educational Research Policy and Priorities Board, as well as with external constituencies.

From: *The teacher's guide to the U.S. Department of Education.* www2.ed.gov/pubs/ TeachersGuide/oeri.html.

Listening 1: Listening for the Key Components of a Presentation

Listening to a Student Presentation

Listen to a presentation about a small study a student conducted on the topic of bilingualism. As you listen to the presentation, think about and answer these questions.

1. Did the presentation have a hook? What was it?

   _____

   _____

   _____

2. What questions did she want to answer in her small study? What key words or phrases did she use to signal listeners about the purpose? (Note: Don't worry about writing exact words.)

   _____

   _____

   _____

3. How did she collect information for her study?

   _____

   _____

   _____

4. What key words or phrases did she use to introduce some of her results and findings? (Note: Don't worry about writing exact words.)

   _____

   _____

   _____

5. Did she give any conclusions? What key words or phrases did she use to introduce her conclusions? (Note: Don't worry about writing exact words.)

   _____

   _____

   _____

Making an Impromptu Speech

You will have two minutes to give an impromptu speech on the challenges you have faced improving your English. It could be about your speaking or your writing or about a miscommunication. Make some notes in the space provided.

_____

_____

_____

_____

_____

Part 2: Language and Dialects

Getting Started

No matter where we grew up, we think the way we speak is the norm or maybe even the "correct" way. However, as we are introduced to more speakers from other parts of the country or world, we learn that there can be many **dialects** for one language. Answer these questions with a partner.

1. What differences have you noticed in the way people from different parts of the United States speak English? What about dialects from regions of another country? Give specific examples.

2. Is there a "right" way to speak a language? In other words, do you believe that there is one standard form that is better than other forms spoken by different groups of people in a country? Support your answer and give examples.

Throughout your academic career, you will have to incorporate information from course readings into your discussions and synthesize it with material you learn from lectures. This unit's reading comes from a textbook about linguistics for future teachers so is typical of textbooks in English, Education, or Linguistics courses.

Reading

Reading about Dialects

Language and Dialect

Most people think their way of speaking is natural, the best way, and perhaps the only way. It's other people who "talk funny." Language attitudes are powerful things. We are likely to make judgments of people based on what they say and sometimes how they say it. When we hear someone talking using a different pronunciation of the same words we would have used, we say that that person has an accent. Note that it's always someone else who has an accent! Accent is one aspect of dialect.

Dialect is a variety of language that may certainly include accent, but dialect also may be defined through its vocabulary; that large item in your living room may be a *sofa, couch, davenport, chesterfield,* or *divan*. People say *pop, soda,* or *coke* depending on where they live. Grammar is another aspect of dialect. The *y'all* of the South, the *youse* of the Bronx, and the *yunz* of Pittsburgh are attempts to give English a second person plural.

Everyone has a dialect, despite the language he or she speaks. What are the differences between language and dialect? It's frequently said that a language is a dialect with an army and a navy. There is considerable truth in that. There is never a good way to differentiate between language and dialect. The largest difference between a language and a dialect is that a language is spoken in a state that has chosen to give it some power. Dialects become languages for political and social reasons, not for linguistic ones.

[Peter] Trudgill's (2000) notion of autonomy (independence) versus heteronomy (dependence) is helpful here. German and Dutch are considered autonomous languages and the various dialects of both are heteronomous. Autonomous languages are languages that have been politically defined as different, whereas heteronomous languages are languages/dialects that have been defined as falling under a common language. Autonomous languages are independent of each other: They have different models and different political, cultural, and economic centers of prestige. Heteronomous languages, on the contrary, look to the same centers of prestige, perhaps to a capital or to a national academy.

It is important to note that heteronomous language/dialects may be full-fledged languages of their own. Consider the linguistics situation of Italy, where the many regional "dialects" of Italian have a literary tradition going back many centuries and, in some cases, were used in legal and political transactions, not to mention being used in the economic arena. However, after the reunification of Italy at the end of the 19th century, Italian (actually the dialect of Tuscany) was chosen as the standard language for political reasons (as well as literary prestige, since it was the dialect of Dante and other famous Italian writers). It was felt that a national language was needed in part because languages such as Sicilian and Milanese were mutually unintelligible—that is, speakers of Sicilian and Milanese could not easily have a conversation. (Things have changed more recently, due to the influence of the mass media, and now dialects are dying out all over Italy and are being replaced by regional varieties that are mutually intelligible.) Thus, it was a political decision dictated by the needs of the new unified Italian state that made Sicilian, Milanese, Roman, and Napolitan all heteronomous languages under the umbrella of Italian.

Variation tends to lie along a continuum—that is, there is a gradual passage from one dialect to the other. This is called a dialect continuum. Usually, linguists distinguish three basic levels:

- **acrolet:** the most prestigious form, used in formal situations, by educated speakers, often of the upper classes
- **mesolect:** an intermediate variety, used in less formal situations, by a majority of speakers, from all classes
- **basilect:** the low variety, used in most informal situations, by the least educated speakers, often from the lower classes

Moreover, people slide up or down the scale, depending on the situation. This is an example of code switching. Finally, we must remember that not all speakers speak alike. As a matter of fact, no two speakers speak exactly the same. Each speaker has his or her own individual variety of language, called an idiolect.

Dialectology of the United States

Dialectology is the study of dialects. Up until the 1960s, dialect studies used rural informants almost exclusively. The idea was that regional words tended to endure within professions like that of coal miners, wheat farmers, and tobacco growers in rural areas. These people have been identified as NORM (nonmobile, older rural males).

These early studies divided the United States into:

- **North:** People here made a distinction between the pronunciation of *horse* and *hoarse* but used the same vowel in *root* and *wood.* A typical grammar feature was the use of *hadn't ought* as a negative.
- **Midland:** There was no distinction in this area between *horse* and *hoarse.* People characteristically said *warsh* for *wash.* The vowels in *due, new,* and *food* were the same and did not sound like the vowel in *fuel.* Other features were *seen* for *saw* and phrases like *all the further* and *I'll wait on you.*
- **South:** This area, like New England, had no *r* sound after vowels. It also used *might could* and *may can* (African-Americans took these north after World War II).

Despite the maintenance of many dialects throughout the country, some linguists theorized the rise of a neutral "Network Standard" as television became more important in people's lives. Dialect uniformity is fostered by mass media such as radio, television and movies, and newspapers, which contributes to a common dialect by providing prestige varieties that people imitate.

The earliest mention of what came to be known as Network Standard was the adoption of Inland Northern, the dialect from the Great Lakes area, which was considered to be "general American." This dialect area is characterized by, among other things, the strong presence of the *r* at the end of words like *car* and pronouncing *cot* the same as *caught.* Why did this dialect become "standard"? One theory is that the Great Lakes region was historically a commercial and industrial center so people moved in and out of the area from company headquarters to branch offices, spreading the variety. Yet another theory is that media pronunciation guides of the time were based on this variety, and radio announcers would have used the guide's recommended pronunciations, providing another prestige model.

The United States is unusual in that it has no major differing dialects. This is because the United States is a fairly new country with a short history. Contrast this with areas in Asia or Europe, where populations speaking the same language have lived in a given area for millennia.

Given the trend to uniformity in everything from television shows to hamburgers, why do some people keep their accents? Part of the answer is solidarity. Several studies (Donahue, 1993) showed that subjects wanted to lay claim to a certain group.

Another answer lies in accommodation theory, which says that people may adapt their speech to their conversation partner. Their speech may converge to minimize distance or diverge to show distance. Accommodation theory is based on a number of theories from social psychology, among them the similarity attraction theory, which basically says that *birds of a feather flock together;* social exchange theory, which says that we tend to weigh the costs and benefits of any behavior; and intergroup distinctiveness theory, which says that people make comparisons across groups, look at socially valued factors, and may try to set themselves or their group apart through language.

References

Donahue, T.S. (1993). On inland northern and the factors from dialect spread and shift. In T.C. Frazier (Ed.), *"Heartland" English: Variation and transition in the American midwest* (pp. 49–58). Tuscaloosa: University of Alabama Press.

Trudgill, P. (2000). *Sociolinguistics: An introduction to language and society* (4th ed.). London: Penguin.

From: Brown, S., Attardo, S., and Vigliotti, C. (2014). *Understanding language structure, interaction, and variation* (Third ed.). Ann Arbor: University of Michigan Press.

FYI: Understanding In-Text Citations and Bibliographic/Reference Entries

In some texts, in-text citations appear instead of bibliographic footnotes. See the examples on pages 10 and 12. The citation in parentheses provides the name(s) of author(s) and/or year of publication. It only includes this brief information because the rest of the publication information appears at the end of the article or book in the Bibliography, list of Works Cited, or list of References, depending on the style (APA, MLA).

The entry usually includes the author(s), the title, the publisher, and year of publication, as shown at the end of the reading. If it's a book, the location of the publisher is also listed. If it's a magazine or journal article, the name of the publication is included with the volume number and/or issue number and page number.

If it's an online article, the name of the website and the web address are usually included.

Strategy: Recognizing (Listening for) and Giving Definitions

Throughout your academic career, you will encounter many new terms in readings, research, and lectures. In many cases, authors or speakers will define the terms when they use them and follow with concrete examples to illustrate the term. There are several strategies they may use.

- Stating the definition immediately before or after the term (often before or after a *be* verb)

  Dialect is **a variety of language that may certainly include accent,** but dialect also may be defined through its vocabulary; that large item in your living room may be a *sofa, couch, davenport, chesterfield,* or *divan.*

- Giving the definition between commas or parentheses (written) or pauses (spoken)

  The earliest mention of what came to be known as Network Standard was the adoption of Inland Northern, **the dialect from the Great Lakes area,** which was considered to be "general American."

- Using key phrases such as *may be defined as, is called, which says that, that is,* or *is known as*

  Each speaker has his or her own individual variety of language, **called an idiolect.**

  Variation tends to lie along a continuum—**that is, there is a gradual passage from one dialect to the other.**

- Listing details, characteristics, steps, or examples

  Dialect is a variety of language that may certainly include accent, but dialect also may be defined through its vocabulary; **that large item in your living room may be a** *sofa, couch, davenport, chesterfield, or divan.*

- Paraphrasing

  Autonomous languages are independent of each other: **They have different models and different political, cultural, and economic centers of prestige.**

Practice Activity: Providing Definitions

Imagine you have to convert the reading into a lecture. For each term from the reading, list the words signaling the definition and any examples. The first one has been done for you as an example. In the last two rows, write two other terms whose definitions are given in the reading.

Term	Words Signaling a Definition	Strategy(ies)
dialect	. . . is . . . . may be defined . . . . . . sofa, couch, . . .	stating definition immediately using key phrases listing examples
heteronomous languages	are	Stating definition immediately
dialect continuum	a This is called	Stating definition
dialectology	is	Stating definition immediately
NORM	as	listing examples
accommodation theory	is based on	listing examples & phrases
Idiolect	called an	Stating definition before the word
Autonomous languages	are	stating definition definitely

Practice Activity: Defining Terms for Others

As you pursue your studies, it is likely that people in the United States will ask you about your field. There may be terms from your own field that would be difficult for others to understand. Think of five terms that are specific to your field of study or a field you know well. Practice defining terms for others using signal words and strategies.

Terms from Your Field of Study	A Definition Using Signal Words or Strategies
Thermal Fuse	prevents overheating
Valve	Prevents the water from flowing back
Electrical Fuse	prevents, overflow current
Filter Paper	To seperate fine substance
Coarse	coarse coffee, The amount or level of grind.

Speaking

Giving Examples and Explanations

Speakers often give examples and explanations to help define or paint a picture for the listeners. Both are important when taking notes because they may be useful for a test or for research. Speakers tend to signal their examples or explanations with certain words and phrases to let listeners know that details are coming. Listening for these signal words can help you differentiate between main ideas and supporting details as you are taking notes during a lecture.

To illustrate . . . .

To paint a picture . . . .

For instance . . . .

It shows evidence that . . . .

Let me explain . . . .

For example, . . .

Let's look at this together.

So that means that . . . /What that means is . . . .

Here's an example to show what I mean.

There is some more evidence that suggests . . . .

This indicates that . . . .

Let's see what other factors may affect . . . .

For the sake of example, let's consider . . . .

Let's say/compare . . . .

By that, I mean/What I meant by that . . . .

. . . you know . . . .

---

shows evidence that playing sports releases stress. Here's an example to show what I mean. You just finish your exam and you did bad, play any sports that you like and it will make you happier. Let me explain. When you exercise, your body produce endorphins. Endorphins are chemicals in the brain that act as a natural painkillers and endorphins also makes you sleep better which reduces stress. So that means that whenever you're stressed out, exercise.

Practice Activity: Giving Examples and Explanations

When you give presentations in class, you will want to include examples and explanations for the audience to make your talk more vivid and academic. Work with a partner. Share what you have learned so far about languages from this unit and from personal experience. Include details. Complete this chart to prepare your thoughts using the signal words and phrases.

Concepts	Examples
applied linguistics	
bilingualism	
dialect vs. accent	

Listening 2: Visiting a Professor during Office Hours

Listening to an Office Hours Meeting (Video)

Listen to a professor and a student talk about a presentation. The student has come to visit the professor during office hours. Discuss these questions in a small group.

Focus on Language

1. What language does the professor use to express main points? (<u>Note</u>: Do not worry about writing exact words.)

_____

_____

2. Do the speakers give any definitions? What strategies do they use?

_____

_____

3. Do the speakers give examples, explanations, or details? Which phrases do you remember?

_____

_____

4. Write any phrases or idioms that you are not familiar with. Discuss what they mean and in which types of interactions they are appropriate.

_____

_____

Focus on Tone

1. How does the professor feel about the student's visit? How do you know?

_____

_____

2. How does the student feel at the end of the visit? How do you know?

_____

_____

Focus on Nonverbal Communication

1. What nonverbal cues are used to show how each participant feels? Are any of these inappropriate? Why or why not?

   _____

   _____

2. Who has the most expressive facial expressions and gestures? Do these positively or negatively affect the interaction?

   _____

   _____

3. Do the nonverbal cues match the tone and word choice?

   _____

   _____

Summary

1. Do you think the office hour was a successful interaction—that is, did the student get what she needed from the professor? Why or why not?

   _____

   _____

2. How does this interaction compare with your recent office hour visits?

   _____

   _____

3. Which of the student's communication strategies did you like? Why?

   _____

   _____

4. Which of the professor's communication strategies did you like? Why?

   _____

   _____

5. If these participants had a chance to improve this interaction, what language, tone, or nonverbal cue changes would you recommend?

   _____

   _____

Part 3: Learning a First or Second Language

Getting Started

Theorists in any field don't always agree, and Linguistics is no different from other disciplines in the sciences or humanities. Different theories exist as to how people acquire a first language (or multiple languages) as a child and how people acquire a second language as adults. Answer these questions with a partner.

1. How do children acquire their first language? Do you believe it is primarily by imitating what their parents say and what they hear in their environment or do you think humans possess an innate ability to acquire language?

2. Children make mistakes as they are learning a language. How do you think parents should handle the mistakes their children make? Should they be corrected?

3. What are two or more common beliefs you share with your partner about language acquisition? What are two or more things that you disagree on about the processes of learning a first language?

Speaking

Intonation with Tag Questions and Rhetorical Questions

Intonation is the voice pattern of rising and falling tones to help a listener understand the meaning of a sentence. Intonation adds meaning in two ways—it shows the relationship of words within and between sentences and it tells something about the feelings of the speaker (*Improving Spoken English,* Joan Morley, 1979). The meaning of intonation is important because listeners need both the "what" was said and the "how" it was said to truly understand.

Intonation (along with stress) plays an important role in questions. Think about the types of questions you hear in the classroom. Sometimes the professor wants you to answer the question, and sometimes he or she does not. Sometimes the professor will pause after a question, which is a clue that he or she does want an answer.

In general, when the professor asks a question but does not want an answer, it's an example of a rhetorical question. Rhetorical questions don't require an answer (such as, *Is everyone here?* or *Shall we begin?* at the beginning of class) or are philosophical in nature (such as, *What is the meaning of life?* or *Why can't everyone just get along?*) and so have no answer. Often rhetorical questions use falling intonation to make it more clear that no answer is required.

Another type of question that relies on intonation to convey meaning is a tag question. Tag questions are often used to open a conversation, such as *You speak Spanish, don't you?* or *You're in my English class, aren't you?* Tag questions can have either rising or falling intonation. The intonation is a clue to whether an answer is expected. If the speaker doesn't know the answer for sure or is looking for agreement, a frequent form of the tag question is to add the word *right,* as in *It's hot today, right?*

- Tag question with falling intonation (speaker doesn't expect the answer, is trying to strengthen the statement, and is sometimes looking for agreement):

  The answer isn't clear, is it?
  That was a great lecture, wasn't it?
  The speaker really knew what she was talking about, didn't she?

- Tag question with rising intonation (speaker isn't sure of the answer and expects an answer):

  You're going to the seminar the professor recommended, aren't you?
  You don't understand the assignment, do you?
  The study group is going to meet on Thursday night, isn't it?
  You missed the exam, didn't you?

- Tag question with rising intonation and the word *right* (speaker is looking for agreement and doesn't expect an answer):

  Everyone is ready for the test, right?
  You all know the paper is due next week, right?
  Doing the extra credit for this assignment is a good idea, right?

Practice Activity: Analyzing Question Intonation

Answer these questions.

1. In your experience, when do professors ask rhetorical questions in lectures?

   _____

   _____

2. Write three questions you have about English. Decide if you should use rising or falling intonation. Then ask your classmates the questions and find out if they think you used rising or falling intonation.

   _____

   _____

   _____

3. When do professors use tag questions? Who else have you heard use them? When?

   _____

   _____

   _____

Research Strategy: Taking Good Notes

In academic studies, you will have to use information from class lectures and text-books (and other readings) and use it to conduct your own research. Taking notes, recognizing the main points, and noting supporting information, such as examples, explanations, definitions, or other details is imperative to synthesizing information with your own research. Before beginning university-level research, it is best to evaluate the way you take notes and analyze whether or not your methods are as effective as those of successful college students.

Practice Activity: Evaluating Your Note-Taking Techniques

Complete this evaluation to get a better idea of how you take notes from lectures and readings.

1. I prepare for readings and lectures in advance by thinking about what I already know about the topic.

    Always   Sometimes   Rarely   Never ✓

2. I use titles and headings from the lecture or reading in my notes.

    Always   Sometimes   Rarely ✓   Never

3. I identify main points and emphasize them by using a note-taking strategy such as annotating or highlighting.

    Always   Sometimes   Rarely ✓   Never

4. I write only the most important information.

    Always   Sometimes ✓   Rarely   Never

5. I note the difference between notes from the lecturer's visual aids or the reading's words and my own notes.

    Always   Sometimes   Rarely ✓   Never

6. I abbreviate consistently using an abbreviation log I created.

    Always   Sometimes   Rarely   Never

7. I write legibly.

    Always   Sometimes ✓   Rarely   Never

8. I organize my notes so it is clear which main points go with which supporting details.

    Always   Sometimes ✓   Rarely   Never

9. I organize my notes so topics covered in both the reading and the listening are coordinated.

    Always   Sometimes ✓   Rarely   Never

10. I review my notes soon after listening or reading to add, correct, or organize.

    Always   Sometimes   Rarely ✓   Never

Use these questions to analyze your questions.

1. Which techniques do you always use? Are there any you never use?

2. Are you doing as well on examinations as you could be? How could implementing more of the techniques listed help you do better with your coursework?

3. Set a goal. Which technique do you want to improve or implement? Why?

Practice Activity: Improving Your Note-Taking

Practice note-taking by completing the activities. If you need to review some traditional note-taking strategies, see Appendix 1.

1. Review the reading on pages 10–13. Take notes on a separate piece of paper.

2. Practice again as you listen to the lecture in Part 3. Use the chart provided on page 27.

Vocabulary Power

There are a number of terms and phrases in this lecture that you may encounter in other academic settings. Add at least five vocabulary items to your vocabulary notebook or log. Match the words in bold on the left with a definition on the right.

_____ 1. . . . as you'll see, especially when it comes to adults learning a second language, the views are often **contradictory**.

_____ 2. One, proposed by **renowned** linguist, Noam Chomsky, is called universal grammar.

_____ 3. . . . he gets his message across. And his **deviation** from the grammatical norm is reasoned.

_____ 4. She is **bombarded** with English all day, and is surrounded by pictures and words on the walls of her classrooms.

_____ 5. Of course, school environments are particularly **conducive** to promoting language acquisition. . . .

_____ 6. But, as with kids, we have evidence that adults actually learn through a more **cognitive** process.

_____ 7. In these interactions, people try to **negotiate** meaning to get their messages across.

_____ 8. They might slow down or speak more **deliberately**.

a. extremely well regarded

b. departure

c. related to thought

d. opposing

e. confer to settle on an agreement

f. favorable or positive

g. with great care

h. exposed to in large quantities

Listening 3: The Nature of First and Second Language Acquisition

Listening to a Lecture

As you listen to the lecture, you will hear some signal words to introduce examples, explanations, and definitions. You will also hear some questions with rising and falling intonation. Use this chart to make some notes.

Signal Words/Questions	Important Ideas

Checking Your Understanding: Main Ideas

Review your notes. Listen again to the lecture if necessary. Put a check mark (✓) next to the statements that best reflect the main ideas of the lecture.

_____ Some believe humans are endowed with a natural ability to acquire language.

_____ Divergent views exist as to whether adults and children learn language the same way.

_____ Mistakes are a normal part of the language acquisition process.

_____ Children change their language when parents correct their errors.

_____ Children develop creoles based on exposure to pidgins.

_____ Exposure to language is the key factor in how well someone learns a language.

Oral Arguments

Some people in the United States believe it should be illegal to use languages other than English in the workplace, in schools, or in community settings, such as government meetings. Some cities across the United States have passed legislation prohibiting the use of languages other than English in certain settings, for example, when getting a driver's license. Other cities embrace multilingualism, providing documents from schools or agencies in multiple languages. Divide the class into two teams (pro and con) and think about whether it is in the country's best interests declare English as the official language of the United States. Prepare oral arguments for a formal discussion or debate. Use the template in Appendix 2 as a guide.

Rapid Vocabulary Review

From the three answers on the right, circle the one that best explains the vocabulary item on the left as it is used in this unit.

Vocabulary	Answers		
Synonyms			
phenomenon	living thing	elegant wording	observed event
astounded	loud	surprised	superb
divergent	adhering	converging	separating
approximates	equals	duplicates	compares to
finite	limited	endless	detailed
innumerable	bound	uncountable	few
norm	rare	deviation	standard
constraints	conditions	freedoms	bans
scenario	exit	situation	problem
abundant	meager	plenty	extra
Combinations and Associations			
draw _____	under	on	by
work out _____	a hypothesis	an activity	a problem
fine-tunes a _____	person	place	thing
pick _____	in	up	by
native-like _____	pronunciation	culture	acquisition
influenced _____	over	by	for
strong _____	dialect	possession	influence
have a _____ at	shot	guess	reach
rely _____	from	in	on
_____ the interest of	on	in	for

⊏╳⊐ Synthesizing: Projects and Presentations

Short In-Class Assignments	Longer Outside Assignments
Examples	Be the Professor
Think about your major or the field you want to study. With a small group, describe the types of careers or jobs that are possible with a degree in that field. Give plenty of examples and make sure to draw attention to your main points by using appropriate language. Then exchange roles and ask questions of your group members.	Imagine you need to teach a concept from your own field of study to people new to the field. Choose a concept from one of your textbooks or a book from the library and convert it into a lecture. Make sure to remember that your "students" (classmates) don't know as much as you, so include main ideas, examples, and definitions and ask questions (genuine and rhetorical) as you present.
Office Hours	Research Theories
With a partner, discuss if you have ever visited a professor during office hours for one of these reasons: clarifying an assignment or grade, getting specific help on an assignment, reviewing comments provided on assignment (for example, comments on an academic paper or presentation you gave in class), or discussing the level of difficulty of the class (if the material is too easy or too hard). Brainstorm a list of other reasons students visit professors during office hours. Include both topics that you have experienced yourself and ideas for future visits. Then create a dialogue between a student and a professor that happens during an office hour. Prepare to present your role-play to the class.	Research a well-known linguist, such as Noam Chomsky, or a popular theorist in your own field. Prepare a presentation discussing his or her theory(ies), who agrees with it (or not), and how the theory or theories have influenced the field.

Vocabulary Log

To increase your vocabulary knowledge, write a definition or translation for each vocabulary item. Then write an original phrase, sentence, or note that will help you remember the vocabulary item.

Vocabulary Item	Definition or Translation	Your Original Phrase, Sentence, or Note
1. acquire	to obtain or gain for oneself through actions	She acquired the skills to be a CPA through her certification.
2. notion		
3. innate		
4. affiliation		
5. mutually		
6. pattern		
7. relatively		
8. academy		
9. optimal		
10. locational		
11. conduct (v.)		
12. explicitly		
13. virtually		
14. critical		

Vocabulary Item	Definition or Translation	Your Original Phrase, Sentence, or Note
15. stimulus		
16. solidarity		
17. aspect		
18. prestigious		
19. emerge		
20. full-fledged		
21. get across (a message)		
22. differentiate		
23. radically		
24. integrate		
25. capacity		

Geology: Natural Disasters

Geology is an interdisciplinary subject that draws on different scientific disciplines. Geology is a science that studies the Earth, the materials that compose it, and the changes those materials undergo. Geologists often study natural disasters, such as avalanches, earthquakes, floods, or volcanoes. This unit explores geological phenomena that can leave great destruction in their path.

Part 1: Wildfires

Getting Started

Wildfires, regardless of how they start, often spread very quickly and burn large acres of land and everything else—trees, grass, and any buildings—in their way. Sometimes when they spread, they aren't stopped by highways or roads or bodies of water. Wildfires occur in many countries around the world; they are very common in the United States, especially in the western part of the country. Although they are usually considered a negative occurrence, there are times when fires are started deliberately in an effort to manage forests or to develop techniques for fire prevention. Answer these questions with a partner.

1. What do you know about how wildfires start and spread? Why are they of interest to geologists?

2. What are some other ways that nature can be destructive? Pick one and discuss how it might be of interest to geologists?

Strategy: Listening for and Describing Processes, Developments, and Changes

It is not uncommon in academic studies to learn about processes, developments, and changes. The language used to describe processes is transferable to many disciplines. For example, in Geology, you may learn about a chemical process that changes the Earth, or in History, you may read about the events leading to a conflict or a peace treaty. Certain words and phrases help speakers connect parts of a process or mark developments and changes.

Introductions

> I'd like to show you how . . . .
>
> There are/were _____ stages of . . . .
>
> What steps should people take? I'd like to provide some answers.

Indicating sequence

> The first stage/step/event is/was . . . .
>
> The first thing to do is . . . .
>
> Phase one/two consists/consisted of . . . .
>
> Initially, . . .
>
> To start with . . . .
>
> Prior to/before that . . . .
>
> The next stage/step is . . . .
>
> Then/Subsequently, . . .
>
> After the initial stage, . . .
>
> When/As soon as this happens, . . .

Describing concurrent events

> While/When _____, _____ happens.
>
> _____ happens simultaneously with _____.

Describing causal relationships in a process

> As soon as _____ occurs/happens, _____ happens . . . .
>
> _____ results in . . . .
>
> As a result of _____, . . .

Concluding a process

> Eventually, . . .
>
> Finally, . . .
>
> _____ concludes with/by . . . .
>
> _____ ends with/by . . . .
>
> In conclusion, . . .

Practice Activity: Continuing the Description

Read the short description from the U.S. Geological Survey (USGS) about its six goals. Then complete the activity.

USGS Geology efforts address major societal issues that involve geologic hazards and disasters, climate variability and change, energy and mineral resources, ecosystem and human health, and groundwater availability. Our science strategy for geologic activities, *Geology for a Changing World 2010–2020: Implementing the U.S. Geological Survey Science Strategy*, presents six goals with accompanying strategic actions and products to further the science directions of the USGS science strategy, *Facing Tomorrow's Challenges—U.S. Geological Survey Science in the Decade 2007–2017*.

The six goals are: (1) to characterize and interpret the geologic framework of the Earth through time; (2) to understand earth surface and climatic processes and anticipate their effects on ecosystem health and change; (3) to understand and quantify the availability of Earth's natural resources in a global context; (4) to increase the resilience of communities to geologic and environmental hazards; (5) to apply the most advanced technologies and best practices to effectively acquire, analyze, and communicate our data and knowledge; and (6) to develop a flexible and diverse workforce for the future. The goals emphasize the critical role of the USGS in providing long-term research, monitoring, and assessments for the nation and the

world and describe measures that must be undertaken to ensure geo-

logic expertise and knowledge for the future.

From: United States Geological Survey at http://geology.usgs.gov/index.htm.

Imagine USGS representatives wanted to complete all six goals in a particular order. Decide the order you think is most important. Rewrite the second paragraph to include language that describes the processes, developments, and changes that you recommend.

_____

_____

_____

_____

_____

_____

_____

_____

_____

_____

Speaking

Clarifying

In group discussions or even during a lecture, you may need to ensure that you've heard something correctly or understand the concept or its meaning. It's a good idea to seek clarification when needed. Continuing a discussion without the clarification may make listening more difficult and leave you unable to participate.

ASKING FOR CLARIFICATION

I'm sorry. Could you say that again?

I'm not sure what you mean by . . . .

I didn't catch that.

Can you repeat that?

Could you spell that? / How do you spell that?

I'm not sure I understood your last point.

PARAPHRASING TO CHECK YOUR UNDERSTANDING

In other words . . . .

To put it another way . . . .

If I understand you . . . .

Basically . . . .

Excuse me, did you say . . . ?

What I understood was . . . , right?

So are you saying . . . ?

Am I correct in assuming that . . . ?

It is also important to notice certain phrases that tell you when someone is clarifying information already given. Use these words also when you are the one giving clarification.

GIVING CLARIFICATION

Let me rephrase that.

My point was . . . .

What I meant was . . . .

In other words, . . .

By that I mean . . . .

I think I can clear it up by saying . . . .

<u>Note</u>: Many clarification phrases start with *Yes, No,* or *Not quite* to let the person seeking clarification know if he or she was right or wrong.

Practice Activity: Asking for and Giving Clarification

Think of a process or event in your field or in another class you are studying. Detail the process in the space provided and make sure you include ideal language from the boxes on page 37 and this page. Then find a partner who has a different major or is studying a field different than your own. Explain the process and be prepared to provide clarification when needed. Then switch roles and ask for clarification from your partner about the process or event being described.

_____

_____

_____

_____

_____

_____

_____

_____

_____

_____

_____

Listening 1: Listening for Processes, Developments, and Changes

Listening to a Student Presentation

Listen to this student presentation for language associated with processes, developments, and changes. Listen as many times as necessary.

1. List words or phrases related to processes, developments, and changes that you hear.

_____

_____

_____

_____

2. Identify places where you expected to hear process or development phrases and did not. For example, does the speaker finish explaining all processes? What process or development language would you add?

_____

_____

_____

_____

Making an Impromptu Speech

You will have two minutes to give an impromptu speech on one of these questions. Be sure that your speech includes words and phrases to connect parts of the processes for your listeners. Make some notes in the space provided.

- What precautions can be taken to protect residents in regions of the world where wildfires are prevalent?
- What are possible reasons residents refuse to vacate their homes when an evacuation order has been declared by the government? What should they do if they choose to stay?

_____

_____

_____

Part 2: The Nature of Waves

Getting Started

Part of a geologist's job may be to develop ways to minimize the devastation of natural disasters such as tsunamis and hurricanes. To help do this, geologists must gauge the strength of waves and winds. During the historic 1969 hurricane season in the Atlantic Ocean, Hurricane Camille had recorded sustained wind speeds of at least 190 miles per hour (310 km/h). The depth of the sea impacts the strength of waves as well, which also added to the extreme devastation wreaked by Hurricane Camille. Answer these questions with a partner.

1. What is a hurricane you remember from the news? What was its name and what details do you recall?

2. How do members of your field measure or name new findings or inventions? How are they decided?

This unit's reading comes from a book that could be assigned in Geology or Earth Science courses or in seminars on extreme weather. It discusses the process and developments that result in hurricanes.

Reading

Reading about Waves and Storm Surges

The Power of Waves

The seemingly simple concept of sea level becomes a lot less simple when you try to define it precisely. Stand at a wharf and watch the water height on one of the pilings. In the short term, wave crests and troughs ripple the surface. Then, over the course of a day, the average level rises and falls twice—a consequence of the gravitational interaction between the sea and the moon. These tides, however, are not the same from day to day or month to month; some are higher and some are lower, depending on the relative positions of the sun and the moon and the inclination of the Earth's axis to the direction of its orbital motion around the sun. And then the weather also has an effect—and sometimes a big one.

The idea of sea level is based on an idealized calm sea—one with no waves or tides, with no wind blowing over it, and with the atmosphere pressing down with a "standard" pressure of 14.69595 pounds per square inch, which is equivalent to the pressure of a column of liquid mercury 29.92126 inches in height at sixty-eight degrees Fahrenheit. Of course, a real sea never conforms to this exact combination of conditions. Thus, except for a fleeting instant every now and then, the sea we see is never precisely at "sea level."

But just as we find the concept of a straight line useful despite the real-life impossibility of such a geometrical abstraction, so does the concept of sea level have its usefulness. By knowing where the sea ought to be, we can separately describe the deviational effects of waves, tides, atmosphere, and storm surges. Such information allows engineers to make informed decisions about the design and placement of shoreline structures from wharves to roads, homes to businesses. It enables emergency planners to define and prepare for worst-case storm scenarios. And, over the long term—decades or more—such information even informs scientists about the conjectured effects of climate changes such as global warning.

Every introductory physics textbook offers elegantly simple mathematical descriptions of wave phenomena—descriptions that apply very nicely to sound waves and light and radio waves, all easily verified in the laboratory. Yet seldom do such books delve into water waves, which are much more obvious to the human senses. And for good reason: water waves are complicated. They behave differently in deep water than in shallow water, they "break" on shores in ways that textbook waves do not, and they create surf and run-up currents that defy mathematical description. They also impact humanity in profoundly different ways than the mathematical ideal waves described in most textbooks.

Water waves arise when the surface of the sea is disturbed, whether by an earth tremor, an undersea landslide, a passing ship, or the wind. As the sea bobs up and down, it transmits the local disturbance to the adjacent water, which is also set to rising and falling, which then sets the water further out bobbing up and down, and so on. In deep seas, the water itself moves in a vertical circle while the energy is carried horizontally in the pattern we recognize as a wave. Usually what we observe, however, is not a single set of crests and troughs but rather a complex superposition of many waves from many sources, all traveling in different directions with different heights and speeds. The sea's often chaotic surface is the sum of the momentary heights of all the waves that are passing through a given point at a given instant. And that pattern is continuously in flux.

Blow across a loose piece of paper held in front of your lips, and the paper will rise into the airstream. Set a wind blowing across a sea, and the water will also rise in a hump—a hump that initiates a wave. The longer the wind blows, the higher the wind speed; the greater the "fetch" (the distance it blows over), the taller the waves grow.

In deep water, a wave must be extremely energetic to "break." And when this does happen, the wave usually breaks backward; that is, an explosion of foam and surf tumbles down its backside. Thus, a ship at sea can usually survive even the worst of storms, provided that the wind and wave are traveling in the same direction (they usually do, more or less) and provided that the vessel can keep its bow pointed into the waves. The ship then rides up the oncoming swell, over the top, and down the backside in the same direction as any breaking water, plunges into the trough (where it may have its decks washed over as it levels out), and then rides up the next swell.

In shallow water, however, the dynamics change. When the water depth is less than about ten wavelengths (the horizontal distance between crests), the motion of the wave extends all the way to the sea floor. Now the wave drags against the bottom, its forward speed decreases, and it grows in height. It also bends (or "refracts") until its crests are roughly parallel to the shoreline, regardless of the direction of the wind. All of the separate waves of different wavelengths and wave speeds that contribute to the complexity of the surface of the deep sea now fall into a lockstep pattern, carrying their energy toward shore with one single speed. And then, when the water shallows out to where it can no longer sustain the wave's height, the wave rolls forward and breaks into an explosion of surf.

It is during its death throes, of course, that a wave does its damage. A wave carries a great deal of kinetic energy, and when such a wave disappears at the surf line, that energy must go somewhere. Some of it is converted into heat, a little bit goes into sound, and whatever is left goes into dislocating heavy objects it encounters—beach sand, riprap, piers, wharves, buildings, roads, bridges, ships.

We humans have a habit of thinking linearly: We go to a beach, we watch what a three-foot breaker does, and most of us assume that a six-foot breaker would do twice as much. Mother Nature, however, is not so simple-minded. Each time she doubles the height of a wave (all other factors being equal), she packs four times as much energy into it. If we compare a twelve-foot wave with a three-foot wave, the larger one carries roughly sixteen times as much destructive power. Large waves striking a shoreline are extremely potent agents of potential destruction.

But this is still not the whole story about waves. In a hurricane, something additional happens to the sea: the phenomenon of storm surge.

A storm surge begins when a broad bulge of seawater, typically around fifty miles in diameter and a few feet high, is lifted up by hurricane-force winds. This bulge follows along beneath the storm, its height somewhat greater in the storm's right front quadrant where the winds are the greatest. When the storm enters shallow water, the bulge drags against the seafloor, slows its forward motion, and the faster-moving tail end of the swell piles over the front end, increasing its depth. Meanwhile, the normal storm waves still ply the surface.

If hurricanes are monstrously complicated to predict, storm surges are no easier. The height of a surge depends on complex interactions between the atmosphere, the sea, the seafloor and its slope, and the specific geometry of the coast. The worst possible combination of conditions is an intense but compact hurricane sweeping into a shallow-water bay—exactly the set of conditions that Bay St. Louis in Mississippi offered to Hurricane Camille in August of 1969.

From: Howard, J.A. (2005). *Category 5: The story of Camille*. Ann Arbor: University of Michigan Press.

Strategy: Activating and Using Prior Knowledge

Many students underestimate their own knowledge. Everyone has some knowledge, however small, about the topics being studied. Activating this prior knowledge will help you understand new parts of the information more effectively and better comprehend what you hear in lectures or in discussions.

Even a very small piece of information that seems insignificant can prove helpful. *To activate* means "to set something in motion"; equate this to turning on a light switch. Sometimes this knowledge comes to mind right away. Other times, it helps to take a few minutes to more deliberately activate your knowledge.

1. Familiarize yourself with the topic of the lecture or discussion ahead of time if possible. Check the course website, the textbook, or prior lecture notes to find the title or general topic.
2. Think about what you already know about the topic. Talking with a classmate about the topic allows you to put your own ideas into coherent thoughts and may provide you with additional information if your partner knows something about the topic that you don't.
3. Consider information you have heard or read before, general impressions about the topic, and questions you would like to have answered. Make lists if writing things helps you remember them later.
4. Think about vocabulary that will be used to discuss the topic. List words you already know, find lists in the course textbook, or conduct a quick online search to find relevant vocabulary. You are likely to hear those words in a lecture. Even if they're not used in the lecture, you'll probably be able to use them during a class discussion or to complete an assignment.

Practice Activity: Activating Prior Knowledge

Work with a partner. For each topic that appears later in the book, take notes on a separate piece of paper about what you already know about the topic and what words and phrases you think may appear in a reading or lecture about that topic. Spend no more than ten minutes on each topic (five minutes for each set of notes).

1. Augustus and the Roman Empire

2. Aphasia and Assistive Technology and Communication

3. Engineering Innovations: Tunnels

Speaking

Discussing New Concepts

In group discussions, it is important to be able to discuss and describe new concepts, as well as understand them when others are speaking. These concepts may be familiar to you and you must explain them to others, or they may be new ideas that you have heard described by the professor and that you now must share. Certain phrases can be used or adapted when introducing or describing a concept that is new to you or others.

DESCRIBING A CONCEPT

The text explains that . . . .

The example of _____ shows . . . .

An illustration of this is . . . .

To demonstrate _____ , the reading says . . . .

The professor meant that . . . .

The text indicates that . . . .

It is often the case that . . . .

Often, speakers will want to let the listeners know that this is a new concept for them as well. To do so, they will paraphrase and make their listeners aware that it is an attempted paraphrase.

DESCRIBING BY PARAPHRASING

If I understood correctly, it means that . . . .

As far as I understand, it shows us that . . . .

So I think that the professor is telling us that . . . .

So what I think that means is that . . . .

The way I understand it . . . .

That means . . . .

Review the paraphrasing phrases on page 37. These might be useful when discussing new concepts as well.

FYI: Reviewing Note-Taking on New Words and Concepts

It's easy to panic when you hear a word you are not familiar with in a lecture. You may worry that you don't know how to spell it and then you may miss the definition. Or you may draw a blank and not know what to write down. You may also see it on a visual and concentrate on copying it, but then miss the definition when it is described or paraphrased. Some strategies for dealing with new vocabulary are suggested.

✓ Write only the first letter or first few letters you know. Then write the definition that the instructor uses. You can look up the spelling later.

✓ Put a star or some other notation by the new word so you can check the spelling or definition later.

✓ Write the word phonetically—the way it sounds. That can help figure out the spelling later.

✓ Concentrate on the root of the word and not the prefixes or suffixes. From the definition, you can determine the affixes later.

✓ Write new terms in the margin so they will be easy to go back and find later.

Practice Activity: Discussing New Concepts

Discuss your understanding of these concepts in small groups using the language in the boxes on page 45. For each one, provide an example or a definition in your own words. Use information from the reading to help if necessary.

1. sea level _____

2. wave crests _____

3. troughs _____

4. "standard" pressure _____

5. deviational effects _____

6. fetch _____

7. break _____

8. storm surge _____

Listening 2: Handling Informal Classroom Interactions

Listening to a Discussion (Video)

Many people believe that academic interactions are formal and that the participants use "proper" English. In reality, many interactions are not formal and the English is very informal. Note the interaction between a professor and three students before a lecture begins. Discuss these questions in a small group.

Focus on Language

1. What words and phrases do the speakers use to seek and give clarification? (Note: Don't worry about writing exact words.)

   _____

   _____

2. How do the clarification phrases start? (Note: Don't worry about writing exact words.) Do listeners immediately know if they understood correctly? Do they get the information that they needed?

   _____

   _____

3. What words do the students use to paraphrase? (Note: Don't worry about writing exact words.)

   _____

   _____

4. Write any phrases or idioms that you are not familiar with. Discuss what they mean and in which types of interactions they are appropriate.

   _____

   _____

Focus on Tone

1. How would you describe the tone of each participant? How does this affect the interaction?

   _____

   _____

2. Do you think the words or the tone should change at any point? Support your answer.

   _____

   _____

3. Who does the best job of conveying emotion through tone? Support your answer.

   _____

   _____

4. The two women use similar language. Who do you think is the best communicator?

   _____

   _____

Focus on Nonverbal Communication

1. What does the instructor communicate nonverbally when the man repeats his question?

   _____

   _____

2. Are the nonverbal cues effective? Why or why not?

   _____

   _____

3. Who has the most expressive facial expressions and gestures? Do these positively or negatively affect the interaction?

_____

_____

Summary

1. How do the students feel about the interaction?

_____

_____

2. Based on the interaction, do you think the students are ready for the exam? Comment on language, tone, and nonverbal communication.

_____

_____

3. What do you like about the instructor's communication? What do you dislike?

_____

_____

4. Who would you most want to work with in a group? Why? Who would you want to avoid working with? Why?

_____

_____

5. If these participants had the chance to improve this interaction, what language, tone, or nonverbal communication would you recommend?

_____

_____

Part 3: What Is a Tsunami?

Getting Started

The 2004 tsunami in the Indian Ocean brought this type of natural disaster into the news and raised awareness about the severity of tsunamis. Although a tsunami can't be prevented, people now question whether some of the effects could be minimized if people were warned in advance of an approaching tsunami. The 2004 tsunami resulted in hundreds of thousands of deaths, perhaps in part because warning systems were insufficient. Since then, measures have been taken to improve warning systems. Answer these questions with a partner.

1. Imagine what could be done to warn residents about a tsunami in high-risk areas. What ideas to you have?

2. What kinds of visuals do you see in your textbooks? To what extent do you pay attention to the visuals in your textbooks? When do you look at them? Before you read the chapter?

3. What kinds of visuals are common with lectures? To what extent do you pay attention to the visuals that accompany lectures (slides)? When do you look at them? Before you listen to the lecture?

4. How or when do you use visual representations in your own notes?

Strategy: Listening to a Lecture with Visual Aids

It is more and more common for speakers to utilize PowerPoint slides or other visual aids when presenting. Visual aids have advantages. For example, speakers tend to be more organized when they have to follow the slides they've prepared. When listening to a lecture, pay attention to the visuals being used to support concepts. Speakers will likely draw your attention to the photo or illustration or to information on a slide or on the board when they want you to look at it. You will hear signal words such as these:

Look at this figure.

. . . which is also shown here in Figure 1.

As can be seen in this [next] slide . . . .

See how this figure shows us . . . .

As this diagram/illustration indicates . . . .

This shows us that . . . .

This slide summarizes . . . .

The results are shown in this graph . . . .

I listed the main points on this slide.

The picture is a good example of . . . .

The figures used in a lecture may also appear in your textbook or in the slides made available to you before or after a lecture. Get a copy of the slides in advance whenever you can and then print the slides so that they are on the left side of the page. Take notes on the right.

It is important to not just write the information on the slide in your notes or to copy only the picture. Make sure to take notes on the additional information the professor is providing. Main ideas are usually written on the slides, so you should list the details that the lecturer gives. Don't draw the illustrations; you can get them later. You'll miss what the professor is saying and miss details.

Practice Activity: Identifying What Should Be Written about Visuals

Look at three slides with diagrams that accompany the lecture you are about to hear. What do you notice that could help with your understanding of the lecture or your notes? Refer to these slides as you listen to lecture and use the space here for notes.

Mantle below crust of the earth. Friction makes the 2 plates stuck.

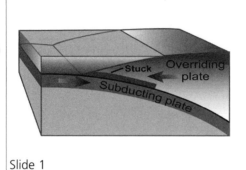

Slide 1

Harbour Wave - Undersea Eq. Huge Ocean waves. 30 ft Sudden movement creates a series of strong waves. Tectonic Plates

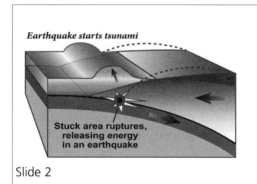

Slide 2

Surface ocean goes up.

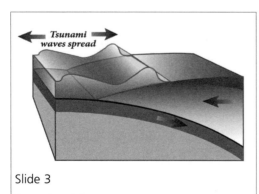

Slide 3

Solitary Waves enormous single waves. Enormous amount of energy. 800 km/h. More than 1 wave.

Research Strategy: Determining the Validity of Sources

It isn't usually difficult to find a lot of sources discussing the topic you need to research. However, quantity is not the same as quality. Not all sources are good ones to read or cite in your presentations or papers.

Some sources, such as textbooks, reference books, or scholarly journals, are usually very reliable. Those tend to be written by experts and the content can be confirmed or has been certified as factual.

Online sources need to be evaluated as well. Pay attention to the type of website it is. For example, a .gov site is a government site and is usually considered reliable. Other domains, .org, .edu, or .com, are often, but not always reliable. A news source like cnn.com is a good source. See who or what is sponsoring or updating the site. A health website sponsored by the American Red Cross is likely to be a good source, but a health blog written by someone who was in a hospital is less reliable.

It is wise to create a "library" of sources important to your field that you can rely on as you move forward in your discipline.

Practice Activity: Creating a List of Reliable Sources

Create a library for your field by creating a list of sources.

A reference title: _____

A scholarly journal: _____

A textbook: _____

A magazine: _____

A government website: _____

An organization website: _____

An educational institution website: _____

Vocabulary Power

There are a number of terms and phrases in this lecture that you may encounter in other academic settings. Add at least five vocabulary items to your vocabulary notebook or log.
  Match the words in bold on the left with the definition on the right.

_f_ 1. The tsunami in 2004 brought to the surface many issues in terms of natural disasters and their impact on developing countries—in particular, the fact that disaster-preparedness or early-warning **infrastructures** are insufficient or lacking in some of these countries.

_h_ 2. Tsunamis were sometimes referred to as _tidal waves_ by the general public in the past, but this is a **misnomer**.

_g_ 3. . . . there is enormous **friction** generated between what we call the subducting plate . . . and the overriding plate . . . .

_b_ _d_ 4. . . . as this blocked plate descends into the mantle, there's a slow **distortion** of the overriding plate.

_d_ _b_ 5. They can **propagate** at extremely high speeds and travel transoceanic distances with limited loss of energy.

_a_ 6. The closer to land the wave gets, the more **concentrated** the power.

_e_ 7. . . . but there are those scientists who **speculate** that animals may have an ability to sense subsonic waves from an earthquake minutes or hours before a tsunami strikes shore.

_C_ 8. . . . but they cannot pinpoint the alignment of the **rupture** that is causing the earthquake.

a. intense

b. lack of proportion; defect

c. break

d. spread or grow

e. theorize; consider it true despite insufficient evidence

f. basic framework

g. resistance; conflict

h. an inappropriate or incorrect name

Listening 3: What Causes Tsunamis?

Listening to a Lecture

As you listen, take notes on a separate piece of paper. Use the space provided to draw your own visual(s) if they will make your notes easier to understand.

Checking Your Understanding: Main Ideas

Review your notes. Listen again to the lecture if necessary. Decide whether each statement is true (T) or false (F) based on the lecture.

_____F_____ After 2004, only countries like Japan knew the devastation of tsunamis.

_____F_____ Adequate tsunami warning systems are in place throughout the world.

_____T_____ More education about tsunamis could save lives.

_____T_____ Most tsunamis are the result of undersea earthquakes.

_____F_____ As the tsunami waves get closer to land, their power diminishes.

Group Project

In the lecture, you learned about the devastation in the wake of tsunamis, some of which possibly could have been avoided.

With a group, think of three ways to better prepare for or manage a tsunami. Share them with the class.

_____

_____

_____

Gather information about how one of your ideas could be implemented and/or what its chances of success might be. Use a combination of research sources:

- interview experts
- conduct a survey
- conduct internet research
- go to the library

After you have done your research and gathered all of your information, create a poster to display your ideas and the results of your research. Consider the list of ideas but also add others if you wish:

- the problem you propose to solve
- objectives of your project
- the steps you plan to take
- the resources that will be needed
- a timeline
- chances of success

Rapid Vocabulary Review

From the three answers on the right, circle the one that best explains the vocabulary item on the left as it is used in this unit.

Vocabulary	Answers		
Synonyms			
subsequent	beginning	following	ending
solitary	lone	withdrawn	neglected
sequence	series	preview	single event
imperative	timely	certain	necessary
simultaneously	before	during	after
vulnerable	powerful	uncovered	endangered
intact	whole	diminished	perfect
delve	skim	view	examine
kinetic	active	elegant	connected
equate	distinguish	liken	guarantee
Combinations and Associations			
raise _____	content	answers	questions
originate _____	from	by	out
to begin _____	with	over	on
_____ measures	remove	give	take
at the _____ time	new	same	first
_____ place	in	on	by
an impact _____	for	about	on
opposed _____	in	on	to
_____ back	washes	snaps	applauds
on a _____ of	digit	number	quantity

⇨✕⊐ Synthesizing: Projects and Presentations

Short In-Class Assignments	Longer Outside Assignments
Teaching a New Concept	Anyone Can Do It
Work with a small group. Imagine you are teaching a class and need to explain a new concept from your field or a field you are interested in. Explain the new concept by defining or giving examples and explanations. Let the "students" ask questions to clarify their understanding. Exchange roles.	Prepare a short presentation teaching your classmates how to do something. Consider ideas such as how to cook your favorite dish or how to make something such as paper airplanes. Include the key components of a presentation covered in Unit 1, as well as the process language taught in this unit. Refer to visuals if you have them.
Activating Background Knowledge	A Formal Presentation with Visual Aids
With a group, choose a natural disaster to study. Take a few minutes to compile what you already know about that type of disaster. Then, individually, conduct some quick online searches to see what information you can accumulate before reconvening with your group to exchange information.	Create a formal presentation, with PowerPoint or other visual aids, to describe a concept or idea from your field. Your presentation should include references to the visual aids and explain new concepts well. Be prepared to answer questions from the audience.

Vocabulary Log

To increase your vocabulary knowledge, write a definition or translation for each vocabulary item. Then write an original phrase, sentence, or note that will help you remember the vocabulary item.

Vocabulary Item	Definition or Translation	Your Original Phrase, Sentence, or Note
1. refuge	Shelter	The wildlife refuge is built by me.
2. in [its] wake		the apartment increased its price
3. remote	controller	Find my television remote.
4. ensuing	following subsequently	The ensuing night, I have a headache.
5. array	regular order of arrangement	He has an array of books in his room.
6. detect	to find out	He detects the smoke from the forest.
7. underlying	lying or situated beneath	He has an underlying feeling that he is lying.
8. abstraction	an abstract or general idea	Its an abstraction of idea
9. compressed	pressed together	The video quality is bad, it seem compressed
10. devastating	causing great damage or harm	The 2004 Sumatra Tsunami is so devastating
11. topography	The detailed mapping or charting of the features of an area	He knows the topography of this area well.
12. fascination	The state of being fascinated	He look at the show in fascination
13. impending	about to happen	I heard there is an impending rain.

Vocabulary Item	Definition or Translation	Your Original Phrase, Sentence, or Note
14. retreated	to withdraw	the Syria Army retreated
15. indicator	an instrument that indicates something	My car's oil indicator is broken
16. slope	ground that has a natural incline	He fell on the slope.
17. alignment	an adjustment to a line	The wheel of his truck are out of alignment.
18. flux	continous change	The economy of a country are in state of flux
19. adjacent	lying near, close	His home is adjacent to OSU.
20. extinguish	To put out a fire	He extinguish the small fire.
21. intensify	become more intense	The situation intensify
22. evacuation	The process of evacuating	The hotel needs evacuation after the fire.
23. conjectured	Speculation	the claims he make is just a conjecture
24. on [its] radar		The school decrease ifs fee
25. receding	to go or move away	He is receding from smoking

Economics:
Inflation and Microeconomics

Economics is the social science that studies the production, distribution, and consumption of goods and services. It analyzes how individuals, companies, and governments allocate resources to satisfy wants and needs. Economists explore issues such as inflation, government spending, employment, and economic growth. This unit explores inflation and microeconomics and their effects.

Part 1: Inflation

Getting Started

In general, inflation is the increase in prices of products and services and the result is receiving less for the same amount of money over a period of time. In other words, what a dollar buys today is not nearly as much as what a dollar bought 10 years ago, or even one year ago. Answer these questions with a partner.

1. What economic forces cause increases in inflation? What are the effects on a country's economy when inflation goes unchecked?

2. What do you know about different economic schools of thought? What factors are thought to impact the strength or downturn of an economy?

Strategy: Listening for and Discussing Problems and Solutions

A common topic of academic discussions and lectures in any discipline is problems and solutions. Problems and solutions might also be a way that a speaker or lecturer can organize a presentation. Certain words and phrases often indicate to the listeners that problems and solutions need to be noted.

Indicating a problem

The problem is . . .

One of the primary causes of . . .

What people are worried about...

Particularly [troublesome/worrisome/concerning] . . .

. . . is due to . . .

. . . is a matter that has not yet been solved.

. . . has the potential to [something negative].

. . . is/was a [continuing/enduring/growing/long-standing/on-going] [problem/issue/concern].

Things got worse . . . .

There were [casualties/problems/issues] as a result of this.

Note that there are many adjectives that can help listeners identify that the topic is a problem, even if the word *problem* is not used.

Adjectives commonly used to describe problems include:
complex, complicated, difficult, tough, enormous, major, serious, severe

Proposing a solution

We can try to . . . .

If we do . . . , then we . . . .

One [solution/answer/rectification] is . . . .

. . . solves/solved the problem.

The benefit of [this] would be . . . .

How about/What about . . . ?

. . . has the potential to [something positive] . . . .

They could/should/might want to . . . .

Ultimately, trying this could lead to [better] . . . .

I'll suggest . . . .

Practice Activity: Listening for and Discussing Problems and Solutions

Work with a partner. Follow the steps.

1. Choose one of the topics to discuss.

   learning a second language

   plagiarism

   fracking

   video games

   email spam

2. Brainstorm a list of several problems associated with your topic.

   _____

   _____

   _____

3. Decide which three problems related to your topic are most important. Devise a solution for each problem. Write your notes in the chart.

Problem	Solution

4. Write a short paragraph introducing each problem and then proposing a solution for it. Use the language on page 62. Review language in Units 1 and 2 and incorporate it as needed.

_____

_____

_____

_____

_____

_____

_____

_____

_____

_____

_____

_____

Speaking

Hedging

In academic settings, speakers may need to let the listeners know how much they believe or are committed to their ideas. In other words, how certain is the speaker about the claim or data he or she is presenting? If there is any uncertainty, it is a good idea to "hedge" so that the listeners know that the speaker is being cautious to some extent. There are several ways to do this.

ADD MODALS

Adding *may, might, can, could,* or *should* can change the strength of the statement.

> Inflation might damage an economy to a large extent.

USE SOFTENING WORDS

Using words such as *rather, probably, possibly, seems,* or *appears* might make the statement less strong.

> Inflation seems to have a negative effect on the poorest of the nation's people.

A good reference list of hedging adjectives and adverbs is given.

Adjectives			
apparent	*open to question*	*probable*	*uncertain*
approximately	*plausible*	*questionable*	*unclear*
more or less	*possible*	*somewhat*	*unsure*
Adverbs			
apparently	*evidently*	*partially*	*presumably*
basically	*hypothetically*	*partly*	*reportedly*
conceivably	*ostensibly*	*possibly*	*seemingly*

CHOOSE VERBS CAREFULLY

Consider your verb carefully. Choosing a word such as *indicate* rather than *establish*, *contributed to* rather than *caused*, or *suggest* rather than *show* work well. Other hedging verbs include *hypothesize, suppose, speculate,* and *guess.*

> I am suggesting that inflation had a negative impact on the United States in 2011.

MENTION OTHER SOURCES

Mentioning that someone else thinks the same thing removes the pressure from you.

> According to some economic experts, it is assumed that inflation will only continue to rise.

Practice Activity: Hedging

Revisit the topic that you discussed for the problem and solution activity on pages 63–64. Answer these questions with your partner.

1. How sure are you that you have the best solutions for the problems?

2. Might there be other solutions? Feel free to add new ideas to your list.

3. How comfortable are you with the solutions you are proposing?

Rewrite your text to include hedging language where needed. Present your problems and solutions to the class. If your classmates have questions, answer them and again use hedges as necessary.

Listening 1: Listening for Problems and Solutions

Listening to a Student Presentation

The topic of this student presentation is Chapter 4 of a textbook used in an Economics course. The content is about the U.S. economy in the 1980s. As you listen, follow along with the student's slides and takes notes on the problems and proposed solutions. Write notes on the lines provided. Then use your notes to answer the questions on pages 70–71.

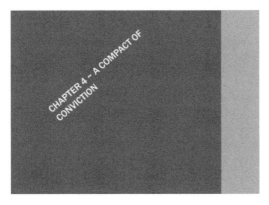

_____

_____

_____

_____

_____

_____

_____

_____

_____

_____

_____

_____

THEORIES OF HISTORY

GREAT FORCES   GREAT LEADER
➤Science   ➤Take charge
➤Technology   ➤Bend
➤Population   events(good/evil)
➤ideas

REAGAN-VOLCKER

Compact of Conviction
Volcker – Chairman of the Federal Reserve Board 1979-1987

➤Raised interest rates

➤Tightened credit

➤Economic slump since 1930's

BALANCED MONETARY ACT OF 1982

Senator Robert C. Byrd of West Virginia
    (Democratic floor leader)
        ➤Force Fed to Reduce Interest Rates
Reagan
    Approval rating
        ➤May 1981 68%
        ➤April 1982 45%
        ➤January 1983 35%

AGAIN THE NUMBERS, NUMBERS, NUMBERS!

1980 – 1981

- Inflation 11%
- 30-year Treasury Bond 13.5%
- 30-year Fixed Rate Mortgage 15%
- Prime Rate 21.5 %
- Industry Production Dropped 12%
  - Auto Production Dropped 34%
  - Steel Production Dropped 56%
- Unemployment 10.8%

LAST TIME...NUMBERS, NUMBERS, NUMBERS!

July 1983

- End of Inflation Assault
- Focus on Recession
- Cutting Discount Rate for Banks 12% to 11.5% (six more times that year)
- Stocks Rose 50% in six months

CASUALTIES OF THE WAR ON INFLATION

- Business Failures 1982 (24,908)
  - 50% higher than since WWII
- Business Failures 1984 (52,078)
- Farm Income declined almost 50%
  - Farm Aide 1985

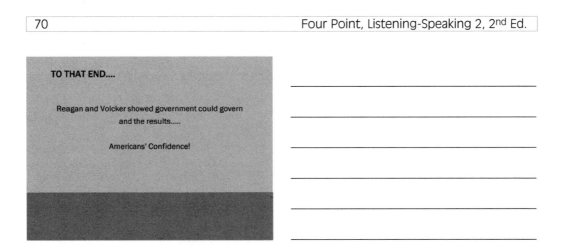

1. Based on the presentation, what were the major problems in the U.S. economy in 1980?

   _____

   _____

2. What specific language did the speaker use to introduce the problems? Was that language sufficient or were there other places the speaker could have talked about the problems? (<u>Note</u>: Don't worry about writing exact words.)

   _____

   _____

3. What solution did Volcker propose and what were the effects of his policy?

   _____

   _____

Slides courtesy of Kathleen Herber. Used with permission.

4. What specific language did you notice the speaker use to introduce the solutions? Could the speaker have used more? (<u>Note</u>: Don't worry about writing exact words.)

_____

_____

5. How successfully did the student present the key ideas in the PowerPoint slides? What would you add or change?

_____

_____

6. Based on this presentation, what seemed to be the views of the author of the book on which the presentation is based? What about the student's point of view? Did you notice the speaker hedging at all? (<u>Note</u>: Don't worry about writing exact words.)

_____

_____

Making an Impromptu Speech

You will have two minutes to give an impromptu speech on one of these questions. Use hedges as needed. Make some notes in the space provided.

- What are the benefits and drawbacks of living in a country where everyone pays high taxes but has full medical coverage and free education?
- What are the benefits and drawbacks of living in a country where people have low taxes and where healthcare and education are offered by private institutions?
- What are two strengths and two weaknesses of the economy of a country you are familiar with?

_____

_____

_____

Part 2: Exploring Economic Issues

Getting Started

Economic policy includes the actions that governments take that affect the economy, such as setting a budget, choosing an interest rate, or deciding the minimum wage. Part 2 covers the confluence of government policy and economic trends and their effect on people's lives and employment. Answer these questions with a partner.

1. What products, trends, and technologies have emerged over the past 30 years and how have they changed people's lives?

2. How do economic policies affect the ease with which people can innovate and create new goods and products? What countries come to mind when you think of the word *innovation*?

In Part 1, you learned about the economic crisis of the 1980s and how President Reagan turned inflation around. Many experts claim that 1980 was a turning point in the history of American capitalism.

This unit's reading is from a book by Robert J. Samuelson, a columnist for the *Washington Post* who writes about business and economics. The excerpt is from his book called *The Great Inflation and Its Aftermath*. This is the same book about which the student presented (Part 1). This book is similar to those that are used in Business and Economics courses.

Reading

Reading about Inflation

Inflation Refashioned

It would be preposterous to argue that inflation alone refashioned the American economy. Regardless of inflation, technology would have advanced. Personal computers and the Internet would have spread. Regardless of inflation, some version of a global economy would have evolved. Recovered from World War II, Europe and Japan would have inevitably become rivals. The notion that America could excel in every aspect of every industry—a common view in the 1950s and 1960s—was a patriotic fantasy. Still, inflation assumed a pivotal role in a transformation that transcended economics and also affected politics and popular culture. In a wise essay [published in 1995], the late economist Herbert Stein cautioned against defining capitalism by a narrow list of economic characteristics. Capitalism, he noted, had to adapt to social realities. It had survived the political threat of the Great Depression and "had gone on to great successes" precisely because it could change (Stein, 1995).

. . . The resurrected capitalism since the 1980s has permeated popular culture as well as the economy. It has altered mass beliefs, values, and interests. Writing in 2004, journalist Roger Lowenstein noted that, in the 1970s, most newspapers "carried at most a simple account of the previous day's action on Wall Street, and television barely covered it at all." What happened to the stock market simply did not concern most Americans. Colleges and universities now offer courses in entrepreneurship, and successful business founders—say, Larry Page and Sergey Brin, Google's founders—are celebrated as heroes. Wealth creation is seen as a vital, risky and, to some extent, romantic undertaking; it is not, as in the 1960s and early 1970s, taken as the inevitable outcome of corporate investment and management. Popular culture and ideas have shifted in ways not discernible in economics statistics (Lowenstein, 2004).

The intellectual godfathers of the old order, [John Maynard] Keynes and [John Kenneth] Galbraith, argued that technocrats could control the economic system for the greater social good. Economists would conquer the business cycle; modern managers would produce technological advances. By contrast, the new order's leading economic philosophers, Milton Friedman and Austrian-born Joseph Schumpeter (1883–1950), thought that economic progress originates in free markets. Schumpeter coined the evocative phrase "creative destruction": Capitalism advances on waves of innovation that, though initially disruptive, ultimately make people better off. The most powerful competition involved "the new commodity [product], the new tech-nology, the new source of supply, the new type of organization." Under the old order, growing national wealth and stability were assumed to be assured and—prop-erly managed—would solve pressing social problems, from poverty to pollution. Under the new order, economics growth was chancy. Because it depended on a will-ingness to invest and take risks, government had to maintain a supportive climate through its tax and regulatory policies (Schumpeter, 1975).

The shift was social as well as intellectual. It coincided with a generational tran-sition in American business that reinforced new attitudes. The Depression and World War II wave of executives was retiring. The early postwar executives cast themselves as enlightened business engineers who smoothed capitalism's rough edges without crippling its productive capacity. They drew their identity from the group affiliation with their companies. Their successors imagined themselves more as warriors and free agents, whose success depended on defeating their business rivals and scoring high on capitalism's standard achievement tests: market share, stock prices, return on investment, and (not coincidentally) personal wealth. . . .

These contrasts emerge in two landmark business books of the past half century: *My Years with General Motors* (1972), written by Alfred P. Sloan, Jr., president and chairman of General Motors from 1923 to 1946; and *Only the Paranoid Survive* (1999), written by Andrew Grove, president and then CEO of Intel from 1979 to 1998. Each headed the dominant company in a dominant industry—cars through the 1960s, and computer chips more recently. The contrasts are dramatic. In Sloan's era, big enterprises seemed suited to serve mass markets through economics of scale in production and distribution. But they might flounder if their size spawned chaos and waste. In the early 1920s, General Motors—the result of many mergers—was highly disorganized. Suffused throughout Sloan's account is confidence that competent management could overcome size's drawbacks and exploit its advantages. Here are some chapter titles: "The Concept of the Organization," "Co-ordination by Com-mittee," "The Development of Financial Controls." These subjects now strike us as dull, but they were real challenges in creating suitable business methods.

Grove (1999) exuded none of Sloan's confidence. Instead, he saw threats every-where, and even when he couldn't see them, he feared they were there. "When it comes to business, I believe in the value of paranoia," he wrote. "The more success-ful you are, the more people want a chunk of your business and then another . . . until there is nothing left." Companies could not flourish just by producing quality products at low cost, or by excelling in research and development, or by expanding into new markets. Firms also had to overcome what Grove called "strategic inflection points"—a new label for "creative destruction." Strategic inflection points are new products, technologies, or management methods that alter "the way business is conducted" (Grove, 1999). Personal computers had dethroned IBM. Containerization had harmed some ports (New York, San Francisco) and helped others (Seattle, Singapore) that adapted faster. People always resisted change . . . .

Different life experiences separated Sloan and Grove. When Sloan's book appeared, the postwar boom was still in full swing, and U.S. companies seemed invincible. Grove, on the other hand, had witnessed successful challenges to many U.S. industries (steel, autos, televisions), and his own industry—on the cutting edge of technology—was in constant competitive turmoil. Sloan wasn't naïve about competition. Too much success for a firm, he warned about GM, "may bring self satisfaction . . . . In that event, the urge for competitive survival, the strongest of all economic incentives, is dulled. The spirit of venture is lost in the inertia" (Sloan, 1972). That, indeed, helped explain GM's later distress. But for Grove, fierce competition was an everyday reality. It prevented complacency. A company might not sacrifice just a few points of market share. It might disappear. Old-style capitalism no longer seemed dated. "Nobody owes you a career," Grove (1999) warned. That was the implicit promise of the old economic order; it wasn't of the new.

Contrary to much commentary, government's size did not shrink in the new economic order. Government regulation remains pervasive. But there was a shift in its role and in perceptions and emphasis. Government became less ambitious, because people lost faith that new programs could solve all social and economic problems. That was a major political legacy of inflation and the failure to end the business cycle. Ideas changed. This was particularly true of economic policy. At the Federal Reserve, Friedman's view that money creation is at the core of inflation became conventional wisdom.

"Central bankers over the past several decades have absorbed an important principle," wrote Alan Greenspan, Volcker's successor as Federal Reserve board chairman. "Price stability is the path to maximum sustainable [economic] growth." Serving from August 1987 until January 2006, Greenspan was determined not to squander Volcker's gains.

Four times, the [Federal Reserve under Greenspan] raised interest rates to prevent higher inflation (1988–90, 1994–95, 1999–2000, and 2004–06). In July 1996, the Federal Open Market Committee debated the nature of price stability. It concluded that, given the technical difficulties of measuring price changes (higher prices for higher-quality goods—say a longer-lasting tire—should not count as inflation) and potential dangers of deflation (falling prices), an inflation up to 2 percent would be acceptable. Fifteen years earlier, the debate would have been impossible. High inflation seemed too intractable. By 2004, Greenspan declared victory: "Our goal of price stability was achieved by most analysts' definition by mid-2003. Unstinting and largely preemptive efforts over two decades have fully paid off" (Greenspan, 2004).

To be sure, the Fed had help. In the 1990s productivity growth was high, oil prices were low, the spread of "managed care" held health costs—for a while at least—down, and stiff competition from imports, reflecting the strong dollar, helped restrain the prices of manufactured goods. One study estimated that all these factors, plus some technical revisions of the Consumer Price Index, might have shaved nearly one percentage point annually from inflation from 1994 to 1999. Good luck and good policy reinforced each other, but the two were connected. The good luck stemmed partly from good policy. If the Fed had tolerated higher inflation, oil prices would have been higher, the dollar would have been lower (and imports competition weaker), and the advent of "managed care" less effective (Binder & Yellen, 2001).

Subsiding inflation that eventually led to a crude sort of price stability was both cause and consequence of America's restored capitalism. But the new economic order also has manifest shortcomings, and just how it might—as Stein suggested—evolve and adapt in the future remains an open question partly dependent on how the American public weighs its relative strengths and weaknesses. Understandably, these issues have become the focus of fierce debate.

References

Binder, Alan S., and Yellen, Janet L. (2001). *The fabulous decade: Macroeconomic lessons from the 1990s*. New York: Century Foundation Press.

Greenspan, Alan. (2004). Risk and uncertainty in monetary policy. *American Economic Review, 94*(2): 33–40.

Grove, Andrew S. (1999). *Only the paranoid survive*. New York: Currency.

Lowenstein, Roger. (2004). *Origins of the crash: The great bubble and its undoing*. New York: Penguin Press.

Schumpeter, Joseph A. (1975). *Capitalism, socialism, and democracy*. New York: Harper Torchbooks.

Sloan, Alfred P., Jr. (1972). *My years with General Motors*. New York: Doubleday.

Stein, Herbert. (1995). The triumph of the adaptive society, In *On the other hand: Essays on economics, economists, and politics*. Washington, DC: American Enterprise Institute.

From: Samuelson, R. (2010). *The great inflation and its aftermath: The past and future of American affluence*. New York: Random House.

Strategy: What to Do When You Don't Understand

No matter how carefully people listen or how fluent people are in a second language, they may not understand every word, concept, and/or idea. This lack of understanding even happens to people in their first language. Reasons for not understanding may include unfamiliar content, new vocabulary, difficulty hearing (due to noise, for example), challenging pronunciation, fast pace, or a combination of these reasons. When you realize that you are not understanding the lecture or topic well enough, try some of these strategies:

- Keep listening and don't let your mind wander.
- Write down as much as you can, capturing as many words as possible. This is generally not good practice, but when you are struggling to follow, it can help you get back on track. It can also be helpful when you read your notes later.
- Don't worry about understanding content (you can figure it out later if you take notes).
- Record the lecture or discussion so you can listen again later and fill in the missing pieces.
- Notice key names, concepts, and dates if possible.
- After the class, create a note-taking chart to organize the key concepts. You will easily be able to see what you're missing. You can then use your textbook, a classmate's notes, or your own notes after visiting your instructor or teaching assistant to help you fill in any missing pieces.
- Listen carefully because speakers often summarize throughout a lecture and again at the end.

Practice Activity: Using a Note-Taking Chart When You Don't Understand

The concepts mentioned in the reading are new for many people the first time they study Economics. Imagine the reading was actually a lecture. What are the key points? What notes would you take? Use a separate piece of paper for your notes or chart.

Speaking

Boosting

Whereas hedging is letting you know the speaker is more reserved, boosting is letting listeners know that the speaker is more confident or simply believes more strongly in the ideas or claims. Boosting can often be persuasive. There are several ways to strengthen your claims.

AVOID MODALS

Avoiding modals will strengthen the statement. Compare these two sentences.

> Inflation may damage an economy to a large extent.
>
> Inflation damages an economy to a large extent.

USE STRENGTHENING WORDS

Using adjectives and adverbs will allow a speaker to show conviction and assert a stronger claim. Examples include *decidedly, obviously,* and *of course.*

> Inflation had a decidedly negative effect on the poorest of the nation's people.

A good reference list of boosting adjectives and adverbs is provided.

Adverbs		
assuredly	*definitely*	*unequivocally*
certainly	*obviously*	*unmistakably*
clearly	*undoubtedly*	*unquestionably*
decidedly		
Adverbs		
certain	*essential*	*incontrovertible*
conclusive	*evident*	*no/beyond doubt*
doubtless	*given that*	*unequivocal*

CHOOSE VERBS CAREFULLY

Consider your choice in verbs carefully as you do for hedging. However, choose the stronger verb when you want to boost. Choose *establish* over *indicate*, *caused* over *contributed to*, and *show* over *suggest*.

> These numbers establish that inflation had a negative impact on the United States in 2011.

USE HUMOR, MOCKERY, OR HYPERBOLE

Using humor or exaggeration helps portray your conviction to an idea well.

> a patriotic fantasy
> intellectual godfathers of the old order
> cast themselves as enlightened business engineers
> personal computers had dethroned IBM
> containerization had harmed some ports

Practice Activity: Boosting

Read the first paragraph of the reading again. Which phrases do you think express the writer's attempt to boost? Underline them.

It would be preposterous to argue that inflation alone refashioned the American economy. Regardless of inflation, technology would have advanced. Personal computers and the Internet would have spread. Regardless of inflation, some version of a global economy would have evolved. Recovered from World War II, Europe and Japan would have inevitably become rivals. The notion that America could excel in every aspect of every industry—a common view in the 1950s and 1960s—was a patriotic fantasy. Still, inflation assumed a pivotal role in a transformation that transcended economics and also affected politics and popular culture. In a wise essay [published in 1995], the late economist Herbert Stein cautioned against defining capitalism by a narrow list of economic characteristics. Capitalism, he noted, had to adapt to social realities. It had survived the political threat of the Great Depression and "had gone on the great successes" precisely because it could change (Stein, 1995).

Mark any places where you think hedging or boosting is needed. Edit to include strategies from pages 65 and 78 and above.

Listening 2: Assigning Tasks on a Group Project

Listening in Groups (Video)

Group projects are common in academic and professional settings. Listen to this discussion about a project. Discuss these questions in a small group.

Focus on Language

1. Why is it important to note that the man on the far left chose the words, *I don't mind checking two.* Later, he says he *wants* two specific countries. Is it okay for him to use the firmer language?

   _____

   _____

2. How does the man on the far left contradict his suggestion? Does this affect the interaction?

   _____

   _____

3. What hedging language did you hear?

   _____

   _____

4. What boosting language did you hear?

   _____

   _____

5. Write any phrases or idioms that you are not familiar with. Discuss what they mean and in which types of interaction they are appropriate.

   _____

   _____

Focus on Tone

1. When the young woman says, *I don't love this stuff* when discussing the research task, how is her comment received? Why? When she says she *likes that kind of stuff* when discussing the data task, how is her comment received? Why?

   _____

   _____

2. One student mentions his satisfaction with the group. Give your opinion of his tone.

   _____

   _____

Focus on Nonverbal Communication

1. How does the nonverbal communication add to the language when the young man summarizes everyone's tasks and then volunteers to do the poster?

   _____

   _____

2. How does each of the other group members feel when the young woman volunteers to do the graphs?

   _____

   _____

Summary

1. How does each person feel about his or her task? How can you tell?

   _____

   _____

2. Do you think one person emerges as a leader? Does this affect the communication?

   _____

   _____

3. Do you think the project will be successful? Support your answer with language, tone, and nonverbal evidence. How does the experience of these four students compare to your own experiences?

   _____

   _____

Part 3: Women and Microfinancing

Getting Started

There are many ways to support economic development around the world. Microfinancing is often studied as a model for economic growth in developing countries. Microfinancing is providing funding or other monetary services to small businesses or entrepreneurs that otherwise can't afford or do not have access to such services. Small businesses throughout the developing world are often owned and operated by families receiving microcredit, and it is often women in the families that are running the businesses. Answer these questions with a partner.

1. What are some obstacles the rural poor face in trying to emerge from poverty? What do you think might be some benefits to providing people with small loans that do not require any collateral, or guarantee, so that they can pursue small businesses or economic endeavors?

2. Why do you think more women than men are receiving microloans throughout the world? What are the possible benefits beyond financial stability for women who receive microloans?

Strategy: Connecting Lectures to Readings or Previously Learned Material

Lecturers may make reference to materials covered in the readings or to previous lectures. Pay particular attention to those instances because this is an indication that the content is likely going to appear again on a test or can be used for a research paper or presentation. Some references are quite obvious, but others are more subtle. It is important to know the name of your textbook and its author.

Direct reference to the text

Let's review what we read about . . . .

_____ is one of the sources that showed us that . . . .

_____ talk about this in the book, right?

_____ showed us that . . . .

You read about _____, right?

Smith mentioned that . . . .

The author wrote that . . . .

I don't remember the page, but read that part again.

Find that in your book.

We're going to talk about the chapter in the book.

As you saw depicted in the book . . . .

Reviewing previously learned concepts

Remember that the premise is . . . .

You already know that . . . .

I've mentioned this before . . . .

You all probably took the course before this one, so you'll remember that . . . .

You can review that in the notes from last week.

Look that term up again if you need to.

The article I referred you to explained that . . . .

Let's review what we read/discussed.

Complete these activities.

1. Look at this excerpt from the lecture you will hear in Part 3. Underline the references to other material.

Ok, we're going to talk today about some of the readings, including the chapter in *Half the Sky*. So, Kristof and WuDunn's book is one of the sources that showed us how microlending has become a powerful system to help people help themselves. They have written that microfinance has done more to bolster the status of women and to protect them from abuse than any laws, right? They wrote that capitalism can achieve what charity and good intentions sometimes cannot. And we read that in other texts in this course too. Okay, but does microfinancing work everywhere?

Microfinance hasn't worked nearly so well in Africa as it has in Asia, has it? What's the problem? Is it because it is still new there and the models haven't been adjusted? Or is it because populations are more rural and dispersed? Or, maybe because the economies are growing more slowly, making investment opportunities fewer? Kristof and WuDunn talk about these challenges in the book and in the video, right?

So, while microfinance has been exceptionally successful in parts of Asia, it remains an imperfect solution. Women's microbusinesses grow more slowly than men's, according to some studies, presumably because women are supposed to work from home and look after

children at the same time—and these constraints make it difficult for

women-run businesses to graduate to a higher scale.

2. Find another example of a way a lecturer refers to a text or other outside source. Use a lecture from another class or one you find online. What words does the lecturer use?

_____

_____

Research Strategy: Using the REAP Method

Taking comprehensive notes in class can have a direct impact on your success with exams, research papers, and class projects. The more you can relate the information to your own life and the real world, the more you prove you are able to not only comprehend the material, but also apply it.

REAP is a method that helps you compile information from lectures so that you can use it later.

Relate, how does this material relate to your own life?

Extend, how could this material be extended to the real world?

Actualize the material, how would it work in the world?

Profit, how would society profit from this idea?

As you take notes, leave a blank page in your notebook to the left where you will record triggers and REAP information in two different columns. **Triggers** are things that will help spur your memory later. It might be a picture; or it might be certain words or phrases that help you remember details from the lecture later when you use the notes for studying or for research. The left side is left blank as you listen. The right side of the paper is reserved for your notes. They should focus on main ideas and concepts. This is the side you complete first. Immediately after the lecture, take a few minutes to add your triggers in the first column on the right-hand page. If you don't do it immediately after, do so as soon as possible. Then you complete the REAP column with the connections that you make to answer the REAP questions.

Practice Activity: Writing Triggers and REAP Information

Choose one paragraph from the reading (pages 73–76). Take reading notes in the right column. Then add triggers and REAP information.

Triggers	REAP	Notes

🏋 Vocabulary Power

There are a number of terms and phrases in this lecture that you may encounter in other academic settings. Add at least five vocabulary items to your vocabulary notebook or log.
   Match the words in bold on the left with a definition on the right.

_____ 1. . . . microfinance has done more to **bolster** the status of women . . . than any laws. . . .

_____ 2. Or is it because populations are more rural and **dispersed**?

_____ 3. Women's microbusinesses grow more slowly than men's, according to some studies, **presumably** because women are supposed to work from home and look after children at the same time. . . .

_____ 4. Remember that the **premise** behind microfinancing is that if people are given the chance to realize small economic pursuits by receiving loans with reasonable conditions and terms, little by little, they can rise out of poverty.

_____ 5. In the Grameen Bank system, there is no joint **liability**.

_____ 6. This social collateral has been found to have a **profound** effect on borrowers' commitment to the group.

_____ 7. You already know that the **advent** of commercial production in the world changed gender roles throughout the world.

_____ 8. There are **enumerable** factors that contribute to the economic success or failure of women receiving loans.

a. greater than usual

b. responsibility

c. improve

d. countable

e. separated

f. something assumed or accepted

g. as it appears, supposedly

h. coming into existence

Listening 3: Is Microfinancing the Solution?

Listening to a Lecture

To practice the REAP technique, take notes on the right as you listen to the lecture on women and microfinancing. Then take some time to complete the triggers and REAP columns on the left.

Triggers	REAP	Notes

Checking Your Understanding: Main Ideas

Review your notes. Listen again to the lecture if necessary. Put a check mark (✓) next to the statements that best reflect the main ideas of the lecture.

_____ Online microfinancing is popular.

_____ Microfinancing is a movement intended to bring rural poor out of poverty on their own.

_____ Literary levels are much lower for women than men around the world, which affects their ability to repay the loans.

_____ Women as borrowers have been more successful than men as borrowers.

_____ Microfinancing has been most successful in Asia.

Oral Arguments

A common criticism of microcredit is that governments eliminate public programs and aid programs because they think microcredit can solve their social problems. From a policy standpoint, it means that microcredit programs can lead to the privatization of anti-poverty programs. This criticism may be legitimate, but only if policymakers use microfinance to replace other programs. Another criticism is that lenders charge exorbitant interest rates, making loans difficult for the poorest of the poor to access. Divide the class into two teams (pro and con) and think about whether microcredit institutions are justified in charging high interest rates to stay viable, providing loans to those who couldn't otherwise receive them, even if they don't reach the very poorest in a community. Prepare oral arguments for a formal discussion or debate. Use the template in Appendix 2 as a guide.

Rapid Vocabulary Review

From the three answers on the right, circle the one that best explains the vocabulary item on the left as it is used in this unit.

Vocabulary		Answers	
Synonyms			
depict	represent	define	twist
apparent	hurt	clear	effective
disruptive	worrisome	sad	upsetting
alliance	alienation	association	compact
cautious	careful	comfortable	corrupt
trigger	cause to happen	allow to depart	ask to help
casualties	killers	victims	damages
mounting	exposing	receding	rising
focal	beginning	center	end
reputable	good	average	poor
Combinations and Associations			
to a _____ extent	great	fair	solid
_____ all faith	keep	lose	win
tear _____	apart	onward	with
midway _____	through	to	after
worse _____	on	off	under
in that _____	light	sound	touch
take out a _____	condition	skill	loan
to be _____ play	on	at	for
_____ of labor	addition	subtraction	division
lost _____ in	faith	ability	time

⇨⧓ Synthesizing: Projects and Presentations

Short In-Class Assignments	Longer Outside Assignments
Problems and Solutions	Research on Economic Conditions around the World
On a piece of paper, indicate a problem. Consider campus issues (for example, parking problems), personal problems (e.g., time management), or global issues (e.g., global warming). The problems should be submitted anonymously. Give the paper to your instructor. Then form a small group with classmates. Your instructor will redistribute the papers randomly. Talk with your group members and propose solutions to the problems. Make sure to incorporate problem and solution language and other language (hedges and boosts or language from Units 1–3) as appropriate.	Form a team of three, and conduct your own research on the economic conditions of a country other than the United States. What is the rate of inflation, national debt, or rate of unemployment? What system of government does the country have and how does that seem to affect the economy? You can do some online research and/or check the library. In teams of three, make a plan for your research and be prepared to give a presentation for your classmates in the form of a poster or PowerPoint presentation.
What Would You Say?	Helping Others Connect
Work with a partner. Find an article from the campus newspaper or a local or national paper. Highlight any hedges and boosts. Decide if the hedges and boosts are appropriate. Are they written the way you would say it? Are there any sentences that contain no hedges or boosts that should? Rewrite the article. Then join another pair to discuss your changes and your reasons for them.	Choose a chapter (or a section) from a textbook in your field or a field you are interested in. Prepare a presentation about the material. Do your best to explain the content. Your "students" will take notes, use the REAP method, and practice strategies to manage when they don't understand. During their presentations, practice the same strategies and any others from the first half of this textbook.

Vocabulary Log

To increase your vocabulary knowledge, write a definition or translation for each vocabulary item. Then write an original phrase, sentence, or note that will help you remember the vocabulary item.

Vocabulary Item	Definition or Translation	Your Original Phrase, Sentence, or Note
1. bond (n.)		
2. ultimately		
3. contradict		
4. conventional		
5. plummet		
6. flounder		
7. inevitably		
8. aggregate		
9. exceptionally		
10. discernible		
11. collateral		
12. irrelevant		
13. joint (adj.)		

Vocabulary Item	Definition or Translation	Your Original Phrase, Sentence, or Note
14. spawn		
15. exude		
16. disparity		
17. summit		
18. complacency		
19. transcend		
20. solicit		
21. conquer		
22. stoic		
23. capitalism		
24. pilot (adj.)		
25. trickle down		

History: Ancient Civilizations

Classics is the branch of the Humanities that explores areas such as the Languages, Literature, Philosophy, History, Art, and Archaeology of the ancient Mediterranean world. The Humanities disciplines cover many time periods, but the Classics typically focuses on the years beginning with the Bronze Age, around 3,000 BCE, through Late Antiquity, to around 300–600 CE, and it particularly focuses on Ancient Greece and Ancient Rome during the Classical Antiquity period (ca. BCE 600–600 CE). Initially, the period's literature was the principal study in the Humanities. This unit explores what Classics scholars and archeologists have learned about sport, leisure, politics, and military life.

Part 1: Classical Civilizations

Getting Started

Some people use the term *civilization* to mean culture. It's a Latin word stemming from the root *civilis*, which means "civil," and is related to the root *civis*, which means "citizen," and the root *civitas*, which means "city-state." Civilizations are often distinguished by their governments, arts, and economics, among other things. Answer these questions with a partner.

1. Some people define *civilization* as having a certain level of culture or technology. What qualities does a civilization have?

2. What do you already know about the classical Greek and Roman civilizations?

Strategy: Listening for and Providing Supporting Details and Evidence

As you listen to a lecture or a presentation, it is important to listen for details and evidence that support the claims the speaker is making. Usually there are words to signal that support is being provided. Being able to identify the main ideas as well as supporting details will be useful when you take examinations, participate in discussions and debates, and prepare your own research for papers or presentations.

Based on the fact that . . . .

The existence of _____ is evidence of . . . .

The development of _____ can tell us about . . . .

_____ reported seeing . . . .

It was _____ that led to . . . .

It is therefore possible that . . . .

It is reasonable to assume from these and other sources . . . .

Studies have reported . . . .

In my experience/From my observations . . . .

There is evidence/details/information that . . . .

There are many examples of . . . .

To illustrate, look at . . . .

This is supported by three points . . . .

Notice the ways that this process can be followed . . . .

Experimental results show . . . .

A case in point is . . . .

We know this because . . . .

There are many variants of these words and phrases. Add others to this list as you hear them used in lectures and discussions you attend.

Practice Activity: Providing Details and Evidence

Choose three sentences from the list. Complete each sentence with your opinion and then support it with details, examples, or evidence. Take notes and be prepared to share them in a group.

1. _____ is the best major.

   _____

2. Good speakers should _____ .

   _____

3. The strongest researchers always _____ .

   _____

4. The best way to stay healthy is _____ .

   _____

5. _____ is a great leader.

   _____

6. The most influential event in current history is _____ .

   _____

7. The most important technological advance is _____ .

   _____

8. All students should be required to study _____ .

   _____

   _____

   _____

   _____

   _____

Speaking

Providing a Chronology

In presentations, academic discussions, and in general conversations, speakers often organize their stories or points chronologically, especially when talking about historical events or processes. To make time references, speakers alert the listener by using signals to let them know the date or time period being discussed. Native speakers appreciate these, especially if they are taking notes. You may already be familiar with some of the words listed; pay close attention to those longer phrases that can sometimes be used in place of the words.

Chronology Phrases	Chronology Words
As far back as [30,000 years ago],	before
In [2013]/[the last week],	during
As we go further back,	after/afterward
Skipping ahead [Jumping forward] to	since
Around 2,000 BCE	then, later
Dating back to / Dating from,	when
During the past 10 years [the last century],	as
Following that,	first, second, third, fourth
It wasn't until	initially
To this day	now
In the [19th] century,	recently/currently

Practice Activity: Reporting Data with Chronology Phrases

Use the list of U.S. presidents to write five chronology statements on page 99. Try to use phrases from page 97 or any others you can think of. Share your sentences with a partner or small group.

SERVED IN 18TH CENTURY

1. George Washington
2. John Adams (1797–1801)

SERVED IN 19TH CENTURY

3. Thomas Jefferson
4. James Madison
5. James Monroe
6. John Quincy Adams
7. Andrew Jackson
8. Martin Van Buren
9. William Henry Harrison
10. John Tyler
11. James K. Polk
12. Zachary Taylor
13. Millard Fillmore
14. Franklin Pierce
15. James Buchanan
16. Abraham Lincoln
17. Andrew Johnson
18. Ulysses S. Grant
19. Rutherford B. Hayes
20. James Garfield
21. Chester A. Arthur
22. Grover Cleveland
23. Benjamin Harrison

24. Grover Cleveland
25. William McKinley (1897–1901)

SERVED IN 20TH CENTURY

26. Theodore Roosevelt
27. William Howard Taft
28. Woodrow Wilson
29. Warren G. Harding
30. Calvin Coolidge
31. Herbert Hoover
32. Franklin D. Roosevelt
33. Harry S. Truman
34. Dwight D. Eisenhower
35. John F. Kennedy
36. Lyndon B. Johnson
37. Richard M. Nixon
38. Gerald R. Ford
39. James Carter
40. Ronald Reagan
41. George H.W. Bush
42. William J. Clinton (1992–2001)

SERVED IN 21ST CENTURY

43. George W. Bush
44. Barack Obama

Example: It wasn't until the 21st Century that the U.S. elected an African-American president.

1. _____

   _____

2. _____

   _____

3. _____

   _____

4. _____

   _____

5. _____

   _____

Practice Activity: Providing a Chronology

Interview a partner about a significant event in his or her life. Take notes. Then prepare a short statement to deliver to the class that provides details about the event. Use chronology and time signals as needed to make the presentation easier for the audience to follow.

_____

_____

_____

_____

_____

_____

_____

_____

_____

_____

_____

Listening 1: Listening for Supporting Details and Evidence

Listening to a Student Presentation

Listen to the presentation. Complete the chart with details about time, place, and sports or activities.

Time Period	Place	Sport or Activity	Details

Making an Impromptu Speech

You will have two minutes to give an impromptu speech on one of these questions. Be sure to use chronology words and phrases and other language studied in Units 1–3. Make some notes in the space provided.

- What do sport and leisure activities tell us about a culture?
- In 1,000 years, what evidence will be left behind to illustrate our current sport or leisure activities?
- If someone 100 years from now found a collection of video games that were violent in nature, what impression would that leave about people in the 21st century?

_____

_____

_____

Part 2: Monuments in Culture

Getting Started

Many aspects of a civilization are studied, but one of the most common is art, which can be studied formally or simply appreciated. Regardless of its forms, art shapes ideas and histories of civilizations from the past and the present. One type of art that reveals clues about the past, especially in classical civilizations, is a frieze. Friezes are sculptured and fancily decorated parts of another object, such as a building, a piece of furniture, or another piece of art (see photos on pages 103–104). Because they are so decorative, they often reveal details about the time from which they were created. Answer these questions with a partner.

1. Name a type of art or a specific piece of art, a technological advance, or a medical marvel that you feel depicts modern-day civilization (or represents the civilization from which it originates). How is it representative?

2. If you were painting a picture of today's modern civilization, what would be included in your artwork?

Often, in academic study, students must read texts and then make their own interpretations about it or make connections between it and the course content or other research. The author of this unit's reading is a graduate student who is making an argument based on what others have provided as evidence for their own interpretations. It examines possible interpretations of the frieze on the Parthenon in Athens, Greece.

Reading

Reading about Monuments as Representations

The Parthenon Frieze

Many scholars have tried to unravel just exactly what the frieze on the Parthenon really shows. Theories about what this masterpiece of architectural sculpture depicts range from a more general view of the Panathenaic Festival, Athens' most important religious celebration, to the representation of foundation myths and more. I argue that a non-specific interpretation is most appropriate in comparison to other theories. I also believe that scholars have been misled in believing that trying to decipher the original meaning of the frieze will yield the only important interpretation of it.

The reason I disagree with arguments describing the frieze as strictly the procession from the Festival is based on the fact that when examining the frieze closely for specific elements of the Procession, as described in ancient texts, one cannot identify many key parts that are mentioned. Pollitt (1972) has argued against the frieze as specifically depicting the Procession by pointing out exactly what is absent in the narrative. For example, in the Panathenaic Procession, men known as the *thallophoroi* carried branches, but the figures identified as such in the frieze have no such prop. Additionally, there are men carrying water jugs on the sculpture when, from what we know about the Festival, it should be women. Holloway, in his classic work (1966), also mentions that several essential characters from the Procession are missing from the frieze, including the Panathenaic ship, and the *kanephoroi*, the girls to whom the great honor of carrying the sacred baskets was given.

In my opinion, if the highly skilled Athenian craftsmen were trying to depict exact scenes from the Panathenaic Procession on the frieze of the Parthenon, they would have been able to do so. These sculptors were able to carve four inches of marble into eight horses abreast. Not only that, but on closer examination, the proportion of the size of the riders to their horses is not accurate; the people are larger than they should be. This effect does make the scene look completely natural, causing the viewer to get the impression that the horsemen, with their heads slightly bowed, are in total control of their surroundings. With the extraordinary skill of these workers in mind, I do not think it is too much to imagine that had the intent been to show a precise idea, in this case the Panathenaic Procession, these Greeks would have.

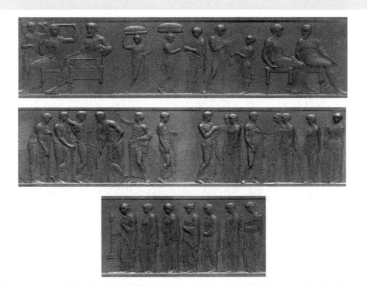

A portion of the east frieze on the Parthenon.

It could be that the sculptors' goal was simply to allude to the festival life of Athens during the 5th century and, in a general way, do so by using images associated with the Panathenaic Procession, a celebration every Athenian was familiar with. I find Pollitt (1972) most convincing when he tries to persuade his readers of this notion. He systematically examines the different sides of the frieze and explains that each element most likely belongs to a wider festival culture of Athens, rather than the specific Panathenaic Procession. For example, Pollitt (1972) discredits scholars who assume that because the cavalry scene is so prominent on the frieze and because the most widely held modern interpretation of it is as the Panathenaic Procession, this scene must have been part of that festival. He also points out that, according to ancient sources, cavalry processions often took place in Athens. Since having a cavalry was a new and probably quite an exciting occurrence for the city of Athens, it would make sense that a procession by this powerful military force would be quite exhilarating for those watching, and even those taking part in it. I can absolutely see why those in charge of creating the sculptural program of the Parthenon would want to include this new aspect of Athenian identity in the repertoire of the temple. Pericles himself said in a speech that one of the three greatest institutions Athens possessed, along with competition and sacrificial rites, was the system of military training that made the city stronger than its enemies. If the cavalry

*A close-up of the Elgin Marbles section
of the frieze on the Parthenon.*

were such a huge part of the Athens of the 5th century, it makes perfect sense that it
is part of the frieze, whether it was part of the Panathenaic Procession or not.

While decoding the exact, original meaning of the frieze as prescribed to it by its
chief sculptural designer, most probably Phidias, would undoubtedly shed valuable
insight into that period of Greek civilization in Athens, it is also crucial to remember
that the monument may have taken on different meanings as time passed. One illu-
minating example of this point is the Statue of Liberty. It was given to the United
States by France in 1886 as a symbol of peace and friendship between the two countries and to commemorate the centennial anniversary of the signing of the Declaration of Independence. This statue stands on Liberty Island in New York Harbor and,
since that time, has been the first thing that immigrants to America have seen. Anyone familiar with U.S. history knows that hundreds of thousands of people escaped
oppressive and poor conditions overseas in the nineteenth and twentieth centuries to
seek refuge in a place they believed offered freedom, opportunity, and prosperity. As
a result, over time, the Statue of Liberty came to embody these ideals for anyone
coming to seek a new life in the United States. So although originally intended to be
a symbol of good relations with France, the statue has, over time, come to represent
far more.

With this example in mind, one must remember that no historical source explic-
itly describes the frieze on the Parthenon. The only texts available to scholars by
ancient authors allude only to the general theme of the frieze. The idea that it depicts
the Panathenaic Procession in particular was an idea put forth within the last few

hundred years. Perhaps the precise meaning the artists intended for the sculptures to have was lost over time; perhaps even the Athenians themselves forgot the original meaning or it became secondary to the original, much like what happened with the Statue of Liberty. What might help scholars determine this is the study of any possible later texts from Athens that mention the Parthenon and its frieze; perhaps clues exist regarding a changing significance of the frieze to the people of Athens or Greece. One thing we know for sure, today the Parthenon and its sculptures hold a significant place in the hearts and minds of Athenians as a symbol of a heritage that has survived through centuries.

The frieze on the Parthenon has been a popular subject for scholarly study and interpretation for a long time, partially because of the lack of any ancient texts that describe it. For this reason, it is an intriguing mystery open to many interpretations. It seems most likely to me that it represents a general celebration of the festival life of Athens, much like Pollitt (1972) describes. Although attempting to discover the original meaning of the frieze is important, I believe that focusing on its cultural meaning for later generations of Athenians should also be pursued.

References

Holloway, R.R. (1966). The archaic Acropolis and the Parthenon Frieze, *The Art Bulletin, 48,* 223–226.

Neils, J. (2006). *The parthenon frieze.* Cambridge, U.K.: Cambridge University Press.

Pollitt, J.J. (1972). *Art and experience in classical Greece.* Cambridge, U.K.: Cambridge University Press.

Strategy: Listening for and Identifying Others' Opinions

Lecturers and speakers often express their own opinions while describing what other sources say or believe. It is important to be able to distinguish what is an opinion, what is a fact, and to whom or what each should be attributed. Certain words or phrases often precede a speaker's opinion. Some commonly used words and phrases are listed.

Speaker Is Certain	Speaker Is Offering an Opinion
I'm convinced that	I find that . . . .
Without a doubt, . . .	In my opinion/view, . . .
I'm positive that	I think, I believe . . . .
I'm absolutely certain that	To me, . . .
Without any reservations, . . .	I'd say, . . .
I'm 100% sure that	To my mind, . . .
I argue that	I wonder / I hope . . . .
I can absolutely see/say	It could be that . . . .

Practice Activity: Distinguishing between Certainty and Opinions

Complete these exercises.

1. Reread the text. Use a highlighter to show what you think is the writer's opinion language. Use a highlighter with a different color to show the writer's certainty language. What words and phrases can be added to the lists?

2. Choose three sentences from the reading. Decide if you think the author is certain or simply expressing an opinion. Rewrite the sentences to include language to make them clearer to the reader.

    1. _____

    2. _____

    3. _____

3. Imagine that you are converting the reading into a lecture. Read one paragraph, and then present the material to a partner. Include language to make it clear when you are expressing an opinion rather than being certain.

Speaking

Leading a Group Discussion and Holding the Floor

Students need to participate in discussions throughout their academic career. Although there is sometimes an assigned leader, everyone can assume the role of a leader at any time during the course of a discussion. A leader is responsible for encouraging discussion, controlling people who talk too much, keeping the group on the topic, making sure the discussion doesn't lag, and providing a summary of the group's decision or work. Certain signals are used to indicate what the leader is doing to guide the discussion.

ENCOURAGING PARTICIPANTS TO TALK

Would anyone like to comment on . . .

What does everyone think about . . .

Does anyone have an idea about . . .

CONTROLLING PARTICIPANTS WHO TALK TOO MUCH

Let's hear what others have to say.

Why doesn't someone else comment on his/her point?

I wonder if everyone else agrees.

KEEPING PARTICIPANTS ON TOPIC

That's a different point. We'd better stay on task.

Let's come back to that after we finish the first point.

That seems to be a different idea. Let's finish up and then come back to that.

PREVENTING LAGS

If no one has anything else on Point A, let's move on to Point B.

We don't have that much time, we'd better keep going.

Let's take final comments on that and move forward.

SUMMING UP

So, we all agree?

Let me sum up.

Leaders must also hold the floor (or help others to hold the floor) and interrupt (or help others politely interrupt). There are a variety of ways you can interrupt others and hold the floor in a discussion.

Interrupting	Holding the Floor
Wait . . . I was trying to say	I was the one who was talking. I'll let you make your point in a minute . . . .
Yes, that's what I wanted to say.	So first of all . . . .
Could/Can I say something here?	Wait, I'm talking now.
Excuse me, can I make a point?	So the other point I want to make . . . .
I just want to say	I have a few points I'd like to make.
I'm going to jump in.	Can I just finish this one point?
Sorry, but I need to interrupt.	I'm almost finished.
I have something to add.	Just a second.
	Only one more thing.

When planning in groups, we need to build consensus and the language we use can go a long way to accomplish that. It is important that disagreement be phrased politely, that we persuade others tactfully, and that members of the group use language that facilitates the group's goals..

Practice Activity: Creating a Phrase Bank to Use in a Discussion

Work with a partner. Think of one phrase to add to each category. Base your answers on observations or ideas you have from personal experience.

1. Encouraging discussion:_____

2. Controlling a talker:_____

3. Keeping on task: _____

4. Preventing lags: _____

5. Summing up: _____

6. Interrupting: _____

7. Holding the floor:_____

Practice Activity: Analyzing a Group Discussion

Think of the last time you worked on a group project. Answer these questions.

1. What one factor played the biggest role in making it successful?

   _____

   _____

2. Who was the leader? What attributes did that person have?

   _____

   _____

3. What language was used by the leader? By the other members of the group?

   _____

   _____

4. How did interruptions and holding the floor positively and/or negatively affect the discussion?

   _____

   _____

5. What other factors made the group experience successful? Unsuccessful?

   _____

   _____

Share these experiences in small groups. As a team, create a brief list of pointers for successful group projects.

- _____
- _____
- _____

Listening 2: Leading a Group Discussion and Holding the Floor

Listening in Groups (Video)

Listen to a group of students as they plan a group project. Discuss these questions in a small group.

Focus on Language

1. What points are the students trying to make? Write the words or phrases they use to help convey each point.

   _____

   _____

2. What phrases were used to interrupt? In other words, what did students say when they wanted to stop someone who was speaking? What phrases did they use to hold the floor—that is, when they wanted to continue speaking? (<u>Note</u>: Don't worry about writing the exact words.)

   _____

   _____

3. Think about the phrase *messing with*. Do you know what it means? Is this phrase appropriate for this discussion? When do you think it might be inappropriate?

   _____

   _____

4. The two women use similar phrases to interrupt and hold the floor. Who do you think is the more effective communicator?

   _____

   _____

5. Write any phrases or idioms that you are not familiar with. Discuss what they mean and in which types of interaction they are appropriate.

   _____

   _____

Focus on Tone

1. Are the tones easy to interpret? What do they tell you about the relationship among the group members?

_____

_____

2. What tone do you think is dominant for each of the four students? If you didn't understand any of the vocabulary, can you tell how each person is feeling?

_____

_____

3. Many Americans would find the exchange between the first two students too aggressive. What do you think?

_____

_____

Focus on Nonverbal Communication

1. Do you think these students have worked together before? What nonverbal indicators (or cues) support your answer?

_____

_____

2. Does the second student agree or disagree with the first student's point? What nonverbal indicators support your answer?

_____

_____

3. What nonverbal indicators does the last speaker use to show her impatience and frustration?

_____

_____

Summary

1. Do the group members agree in the end? What verbal and nonverbal indicators can you use as evidence?

   _____

   _____

2. Based on this interaction, how do you think the next meeting will go?

   _____

   _____

Part 3: The Emergence of the Roman Empire

Getting Started

Many people define civilizations as societies that are advanced or developed in some way, whether that be through literacy, arts, sports, or a military. The Roman Empire has been studied as one of the world's greatest civilizations, in large part due to its influence on the countries it conquered. Answer these questions with a partner.

1. What do you know about life in the Roman Empire? How far reaching was the Roman Empire?

2. What are other empires of note throughout history and the world? What do you know about them and what has been their legacy?

Strategy: Listening to Lecture Introductions

Lecturers sometimes begin their lectures with signals to prepare the listeners and/or provide key information about the lecture they are about to give. Some lecturers tell the listeners what the topic will be and may even give an idea of how the lecture will be organized, especially if the class is starting a new topic. At some point during the lecture, often as part of the introduction, lecturers let the listeners know if there is a reading from the textbook and/or other sources that will be referenced or are related to the lecture (see page 83). Additionally, they may link information from the lecture to previous lectures (see page 83). Last, a lecture introduction will sometimes include ideas about what the instructor is expecting the students to learn. Lectures use signals to guide the listeners.

Some signals that may introduce a topic

What I want to do today . . . .

We'll look at . . . . and then we'll look at . . . .

The main points of this lecture are . . . .

Some references to readings and previous material

We ended last time with . . . .

As we have seen . . . . (signals previous learning; if you are uncertain, go back to earlier notes)

As we've seen repeatedly . . . . (signals important themes for the class)

In the readings/textbook . . . . or As you have read . . . . (signals an expectation to compare this lecture to your reading notes)

Remember that . . . .

We want to take a few steps back . . . .

Some references to class expectations and future tests

_____ has a tendency to show up on the exams.

You will not be tested on . . .

The bulk of the material in this course will . . . .

Get in the habit of . . . .

Some signals to indicate how a lecture is organized

We'll begin by reviewing the history from the beginning of the 1940s through the 1950s. (chronological)

We'll talk about how the Romans and the Greeks managed their economy. (compare/contrast)

We'll cover the most important features of the circuit. (prioritizing)

Today's lecture will discuss how the mechanisms work. (process)

Practice Activity: Analyzing an Introduction

Read the first part of the introduction to the lecture for this unit. Then analyze the introduction by following the steps.

1. Highlight the signal introducing the topic.

2. Circle the signal that refers to previous material.

3. Underline the references to class expectations.

4. Double underline the words that indicate how the lecture will be organized. What is the organizational pattern likely to be?

> What I want to do today is to continue on through our rapid tour of Roman history from the foundation of the city to the reign of Augustus. Remember that Augustus was the founder of the Roman Empire and its first Emperor, ruling from 27 BCE until his death in 14 CE. Again, you will find a few of the names that I am mentioning and going on about on your list for this Friday, the quiz, which, just to repeat: there will be ten short answer questions taken off of that list. The TAs will be going over this at the end of class today. The names and concepts on that list are, of course, fairly central to things that I have been talking about in the lectures, and it will enable me to, uh, see how people are doing with the content.

Research Strategy: Types of Sources

In research, students must conduct research using two types of sources: primary and secondary.

Primary research collects data for papers from "original" sources. For example, data may come from a survey given to a certain number of subjects, from an interview with an expert on the topic, or from results compiled from an experiment you conduct on your own.

Secondary research includes facts and data from "outside" sources. Information may be found in books or journals, on websites, or from official documents from organizations or other sources.

The presentation you heard in Part 1 of Unit 1 discussed primary research. The presenter had interviewed people to gather her data. The research the graduate student conducted in the reading in Part 2 of Unit 2 is a good example of secondary research. She had read about what other people said and summarized it.

Whenever possible, it is best to include a blend of both primary and secondary sources. They can complement each other, provide support, and allow you to offer interpretations. The students in the video in Part 2 of Unit 3 discuss both primary and secondary sources.

Practice Activity: Creating a Resource List

Complete these steps about your own field or a field you are interested in pursuing.

1. What are ways I can conduct primary research in my field?

   _____

   _____

2. What are good secondary sources in my field?

   _____

   _____

Vocabulary Power

There are a number of terms and phrases in this lecture that you may encounter in other academic settings. Add at least five vocabulary items to your vocabulary notebook or log.
Match the words or phrases in bold with the definition on the right.

_____ 1. This document is the political **testament**, essentially, of the emperor Augustus.

_____ 2. One of the keys to the collapse of the Roman democracy is, quite **plainly**, that people were distinctly unhappy with it.

_____ 3. This leads to the rise of individuals with enormous power, where an individual can command so much support within the state that the **apparatus** of the state cannot take any action against that individual.

_____ 4. . . . what it tells us about Augustus, what it is a piece of **propaganda** . . . .

_____ 5. First and foremost, the rest of what you will read in this course presumes that you have a **fairly** clear idea of when the emperor Augustus lived.

_____ 6. But this is the critical and **pivotal** period in Roman history where we see this transformation from democracy to monarchy.

_____ 7. And those states retain their traditions, and those traditions will sometimes shape the broader **spectrum** of Roman culture.

_____ 8. Very often non-Roman traditions and non-Roman ideas will **supersede** ideas that emerged in Italy and will become more powerful than ideas that emerged in Italy.

a. of utmost importance

b. biased information

c. organization; system

d. evidence or proof

e. take the place of

f. somewhat

g. full range

h. simply

Listening 3: Augustus and the Roman Empire

Listening to a Lecture

As you listen to the lecture, note the signals that introduce the topic and indicate chronology, and use them to form the basis of your outline or note structure. Use whatever note-taking organization strategy works best for you.

_____

_____

_____

_____

_____

_____

_____

_____

Checking Your Understanding: Main Ideas

Review your notes. Listen again to the lecture if necessary. Decide whether each statement is true (T) or false (F) based on the lecture.

_____ Ancient documents are an important source of historical information.

_____ The Roman empire was built to encourage economic expansion.

_____ The collapse of Roman democracy was due to public dissatisfaction.

_____ The traditions of Rome superseded the traditions of all its conquered states.

_____ If not for Sulla, there would have been no Augustus.

Panel Discussion

The lecturer talks about the influence of one ruler on a civilization. In teams of three, do some light research to find other examples throughout the world and throughout history that show the influence of one particular ruler on a given civilization or period of history. Examples of possible rulers/leaders are Charlemagne, Ferdinand and Isabella of Spain, Peter the Great, Queen Elizabeth I, Queen Victoria, Kubla Khan, and Genghis Khan. Keep in mind that an influential ruler doesn't necessarily imply that every way he or she influenced the world was always positive.

Each panelist will do research on the chosen topic and present as if he/she were an expert in this topic. The panelists may have opposing views or may present as a team. Each panelist should speak for at least five minutes. Afterward, the rest of the class will ask the panelists questions.

Topic: _____

Team member responsibilities (which aspects of the topic is each going to research):

_____

_____

_____

_____

Questions for other panelists:

_____

_____

_____

_____

Rapid Vocabulary Review

From the three answers on the right, circle the one that best explains the vocabulary item on the left as it is used in this unit.

Vocabulary	Answers		
Synonyms			
central	trivial	key	famous
unsubtle	covert	stubborn	obvious
composed	depicted	equated	prepared
presume	cover	astound	suppose
foremost	greatest	minor	influential
in a row	consecutively	wisely	approximately
revolution	uprising	weapon	promise
conquest	trimming	freeing	overpowering
acquire	convince	obtain	defend
retain	elect	keep	prevent
Combinations and Associations			
have a _____	sight	eye	look
get into the _____	habit	custom	pattern
a _____ deal	lot	great	much
political _____	unrest	ease	agitation
_____ steps	get	make	take
reflection _____	to	of	in
makes _____	understanding	process	sense
_____ in mind	keep	stop	think
_____ a doubt	with	within	without
to make a long story _____	latter	short	entirely

⇨✕⇦ Synthesizing: Projects and Presentations

Short In-Class Assignments	Longer Outside Assignments
Introductions	**Your Own Civilization**
Take the first paragraph from a chapter in a textbook you are using in another class or find one in the library. Write an introduction as if you had to present the material as a lecture. Present it to your classmates.	Choose a civilization to study. What was happening in the 3rd century BCE and the 3rd century CE? Conduct some research for details and evidence about those developments. You may work with others in class with similar topics. Present what you found to others in class using appropriate language from this unit and Units 1–3. Consider one of these topics or one of your own. • the history of medical practices • the history of early technologies • the history of marital customs • the history family structures • the history of early forms of government • _____ • _____
Leading a Discussion	**Timeline Posters**
Choose a topic of interest from the campus newspaper or a current event to discuss with your group. Lead the group in discussing the topic for five minutes. Employ the strategies detailed on pages 107–108. Exchange roles. Remember that all the responsibility does not belong to the leader. When you are a participant, do your best to participate actively, especially when the leader calls on you.	Choose an event or discovery that is important to your field. Prepare a poster presentation that provides an accurate chronology of the event or discovery. Be prepared to offer explanations as to why this event or discovery was important to the field. Use appropriate words and phrases so your listeners will be able to tell when you are certain about information and when you are simply offering an opinion. Be prepared to present your poster to the class on the assigned day.

Vocabulary Log

To increase your vocabulary knowledge, write a definition or translation for each vocabulary item. Then write an original phrase, sentence, or note that will help you remember the vocabulary item.

Vocabulary Item	Definition or Translation	Your Original Phrase, Sentence, or Note
1. voluntary		
2. representative		
3. regulated		
4. attribute (n.)		
5. reign		
6. distinctly		
7. imperial		
8. broadly		
9. digress		
10. phase		
11. hand in hand		
12. enable		
13. unprecedented		
14. republic		

Vocabulary Item	Definition or Translation	Your Original Phrase, Sentence, or Note
15. intended		
16. in large measure		
17. established		
18. consequences		
19. assimilate		
20. spectacle		
21. resemble		
22. excavation		
23. unravel		
24. spectator		
25. allude to		

5

Health Sciences: Neurological Disorders

A neurological disorder is one that impacts the body's nervous system; it occurs when the membranes around the brain and spinal cord are affected. Neurological conditions are fairly common and millions of people across the globe have experienced some sort of neurological condition. Some common disorders include migraines or back pain. This unit will explore neurological conditions, their prevalence, how those with certain conditions are viewed across cultures, and the services that are provided for those affected.

Part 1: Strokes

Getting Started

Strokes occur when the blood supply to the brain is disrupted and brain function is lost. Several events may cause the disruption, and different parts of the brain may be affected. Depending on which part of the brain is affected, the stroke victim may not be able to move one side of his or her body, speak, or see well.

1. In general, what are some things people can do to promote good health?

2. What do you know about strokes? Have you ever known anyone who has had a stroke? What were they like before and after the stroke?

3. Some neurological conditions are preventable. What do you think can be done to avoid a stroke?

Strategy: Listening for and Talking about Statistics and Trends

Every field has statistics of some type. As a result, many academic talks contain statistics. Speakers use a variety of phrases to show trends, increases, or decreases in numbers or figures. It is important to note that these concepts may be more important than the specific numbers.

> In the United States, more than 140,000 people die each year from stroke, making it the third leading cause of death in the United States.

> There have been some positive trends in developed countries, where the incidence of stroke is declining.

Showing Trends	Showing Increases	Showing Decreases
A considerable number of . . .	_____ has increased 3-fold. (multiplied by 3)	_____ has decreased 4-fold. (multiplied by 4)
A large proportion of . . .	_____ has decreased significantly.	_____ has decreased significantly.
Most people . . .	There's been a considerable increase in	There's been a considerable decrease in . . . .
The majority . . .		
The vast majority . . .	There's been a substantial increase in	There's been a substantial increase in . . . .
. . . each year.		
. . . making it the third leading [cause] . . .	The number of _____ has skyrocketed.	The number of _____ has plummeted.
Nearly all . . .	. . . is increasing.	. . . is declining.
Most of . . .		
The most common . . .	A higher incidence . . .	Fewer incidents are occuring.
. . . can be expanded.	. . . a higher [rate of] incidence.	. . . a lower [rate of] incidence.
. . . occurs every [3 years].	There is a greater risk	There is less risk . . . .

Practice Activity: Talking about Statistics

Look at the figure here and the table on page 126 regarding the hospitalization rates for stroke victims over the age of 65. Write some statements about the statistics. Notice trends, increases, and decreases. One example has been done for you.

Figure 5.1. Hospitalization Rates for Stroke for Those Aged 65 and Over: United States, 1989, 1999, and 2009

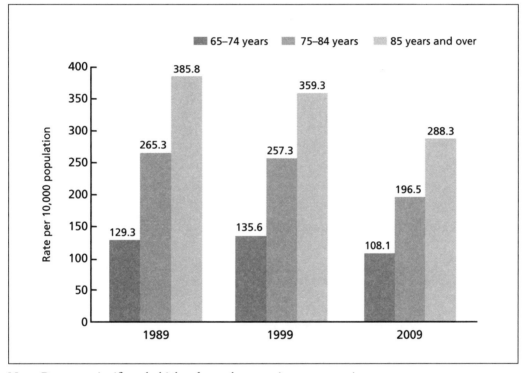

Note: Rates are significantly higher for each successive age group in every year.

From: CDC/NCHS, National Hospital Discharge Survey, 1989, 2999, and 2009, www.cdc.gov/nchs/data/databriefs/db95.htm#rate.

The rate of hospitalization for stroke victims older than 85 was almost three times

the rate of victims in the 65–74 age range in 1989.

_____

_____

_____

_____

Table 5.1. Number and Characteristics of Hospitalizations for Stroke:
United States, 1989, 1999, and 2009

Characteristic	1989	1999	2009
Total stroke hospitalizations	795,000	961,000	971,000
Average age of hospital inpatients (years)	71	71	70
Proportion by Sex	Percent		
Male	43	45	48
Female	57	55	52
Proportion by Age Group			
Under 65 years	24	27	34
65 years and over	76	73	66
Proportion with Comorbidities			
Diabetes	18	23	23
Hypertension	37	55	58
Atrial fibrillation	10	12	12
At least one of the above comorbidities[1]	65	91	94

[1]Percentage of stroke inpatients with one or more of the above comorbidities in diagnostic fields 2 through 7 on the National Hospital Discharge Survey patient medical abstract form, according to the CDC.
From: CDC/NCHS, National Hospital Discharge Survey, 1989, 1999, and 2009, www.cdc.gov/nchs/data/databriefs/db95.htm#rate.

_____

_____

_____

_____

_____

_____

Speaking

Presenting Proposals

Presenting proposals in academia happens frequently and in different forms. One version of a proposal is suggesting a solution during an academic discussion. Other proposals are much more formal, such as proposing an idea for a project or for a session at a conference. Some language is indicative of a speaker making a proposal.

We think that if we try . . . .

We believe that [X] might provide [X].

We propose to . . . .

Our proposal/idea is to . . . .

We think it would be a good idea to . . . .

We believe that [X] would solve the problem of [X].

Our research is designed to learn . . . .

Moving forward with this idea would . . . .

It is generally felt that . . . ; therefore, our design will . . . .

We feel that . . . .

We intend to learn . . . .

Practice Activity: Presenting a Proposal

Work with a small group. Imagine a medical foundation has $50,000 in grant money for researchers studying psychological disorders. Follow the steps.

1. Discuss this list of psychological disorders. Conduct some quick online searches and use your own prior knowledge to choose which one would be best to research in more depth. Feel free to choose a disorder that is not on the list.

Alzheimer's disease	Parkinson's disease
childhood anemia	pyromania
kleptomania	a sleep disorder
night eating syndrome	an eating disorder

2. Prepare a short presentation proposing the psychological disorder of your choice to the other groups. Explain why you think this is the disorder the medical foundation should study.

3. Present your proposal to the other groups.

Listening 1: Listening for Statistics and General Information

Listening to a Student Presentation

Many students are required, at some point in their academic or professional career, to give an overview of a topic. This presentation is an informational presentation about strokes. As you listen, take notes on the statistics as well as the main points and other key components. Use a separate sheet of paper if necessary.

_____

_____

_____

_____

_____

_____

Making an Impromptu Speech

You will have two minutes to give an impromptu speech presenting your arguments for one of these topics. Make some notes in the space provided.

- the argument for or against foreign language [or another discipline] requirements at the university level
- supporting or not supporting a current political issue
- describing solutions to a current problem at the school [examples: limited parking options, crowded cafeterias, or closed classes]

_____

_____

_____

Part 2: Autism across the World

Getting Started

Autism consists of a spectrum of conditions, which specialists call autism spectrum disorders (ASD). Its causes are not completely understood. In general, the process the brain uses to understand information is affected by the way nerve cells and their synapses connect and organize information. People with autism usually exhibit abnormal behaviors before the age of three in one of more of these areas: (1) social interaction; (2) communication; or (3) restricted interests and activities.

Several of the following social problems can be present in people with an autistic disorder: inappropriate use of nonverbal communication, difficulty in peer relations, lack of social-emotional connections, and lack of shared enjoyment. Those with autism may fail to develop speech and face difficulties sustaining conversations. They may have an unusual preoccupation with narrow interests or objects and may tend to be inflexible and in need of routine. Answer these questions with a partner.

1. What have you heard about possible causes for the increase in the diagnosis of autism throughout the world? What do you think might be some causes?

2. Why might a family choose not to give their children immunizations for serious, communicable diseases such as mumps, measles, and rubella? What is the danger to a community if families choose not to vaccinate their infants and children?

Some people believe that there is a connection between childhood vaccinations and the increased incidence of autism. When reading about research findings, you will typically be looking for a hypothesis, results, and discussion. Prepare an outline using these categories and take notes as you read. Depending on the discipline, you may also see an introduction or conclusion, or other sections. This unit's reading comes from a research paper written by a graduate student.

Reading

Reading about Autism and Vaccines

Autism and Vaccines: Where Does the Evidence Stand?

In the past 20 years, the prevalence of autism has on the surface increased dramatically. The Centers for Disease Control (CDC, 2007) has reported that 1 in 150 children have a diagnosis of autism. This prevalence is controversial, however, since some experts question whether more children actually are autistic or whether the diagnostic criteria for autism have expanded, encompassing more children (CDC, 2007; Taylor, 2006). Nonetheless, fervor has developed among many parents and certain health care professionals that this increase in prevalence may be associated with childhood vaccinations (Autism Research Institute [ARI], 2005). This paper reviews current research to determine if any causal relationship has been found between autism and vaccines.

The CDC (2007) has defined autism as a "neurodevelopmental disorder marked by deficiencies in social and language skills combined with unusual interests and behaviors." Autism is thought to exist on a continuum with some children reasonably functional and others strikingly disabled. At one time, autism was considered a purely psychiatric disorder; currently, a gene-environment interaction is thought to be associated with the development of autism. Some children with autism have associated medical diagnoses such as Fragile X and mitochondrial disorders. Developmental and communication regression is often sudden and is likely to develop before the age of 3 years. Because there are no tests available to diagnose autism, physicians must base a diagnosis on specific behaviors (CDC, 2007).

Vaccines as a cause of autism was suggested as early as 1995 by the ARI (2002), a group comprised of parents and professionals whose self-reported mission is to improve the methods of diagnosing, treating, and preventing autism (ARI, 2008). The ARI's (2002) concerns with vaccines have addressed two areas: vaccines containing the mercury-based preservative thimerosal[1] and the Mumps, Measles, and Rubella (MMR) vaccine. However, research on both sides of the issue continues to be unsatisfactory due to the reported poor quality of most studies (Demicheli, Jefferson, Rivetti, & Price, 2008; Parker, Schwartz, Todd, & Pickering, 2004).

[1]Thimerosal is an organomercurial compound composed of 30 percent mercury.

The apparent increase in autism diagnoses coincided with the burgeoning aware-ness of the dangers of environmental mercury in the 1990s and the increase in the number of vaccines children received (Baker, 2008). In turn, as parents grasped for reasons why autism was so prevalent, a comparison was made between methylmer-cury and ethylmercury. Although no evidence was produced indicating that thimerosal was dangerous, leading government agencies and the American Academy of Pediatrics (AAP) recommended removal of thimerosal from vaccines based on the EPA guidelines for methylmercury exposure safety limits (Baker, 2008). Interestingly, despite thimerosal's progressive removal from vaccines (except the influenza vaccine) based on the recommendation of the Federal Drug Administration, the CDC, the AAP, and the National Institute of Health, among others, autism rates have not decreased (CDC, 2007; Schechter & Grether, 2008).

Heron and Golding (2004) conducted a longitudinal study in the United Kingdom on a large sample of children (n = 12,956) with most (n = 12,810) receiving three doses of immunizations and the rest (n = 146) receiving zero to two doses of immunizations at two, four, and six months of age. The results were adjusted for birth weight, gen-der, gestation, and breastfeeding. The researchers found an interesting relationship between those receiving thimerosal-containing vaccines and beneficial behaviors, including motor development, speech, and activity levels that persisted even after the results were adjusted. They reported that only one in 69 resulted in developmen-tal problems consistent with their hypothesis while eight in 69 demonstrated benefi-cial developmental effects.

A study by Thompson et al. (2007) replicated similar beneficial outcomes of thimerosal-containing vaccines in a study of 1,047 children. The researchers also conducted a cohort study where they administered a battery of 42 neuropsychologi-cal tests to children aged seven to 10 years. They reported that increased mercury exposure from immunizations obtained in the first seven months of life was linked to better outcomes on some measures of fine motor coordination, attention, and execu-tive functioning. They found no causal relationship between thimerosal-containing vaccines and neuropsychological dysfunction.

Geier and Geier (2004) conducted an ecological study of the Vaccine Adverse Event Reporting System (VAERS) from 1991 to 2004 to determine if there were any changes in the number of neurodevelopmental disorders reported, including autism, since the removal of thimerosal from vaccines. The researchers concluded that there was a significant downward trend observed in reported neurodevelopmental disor-ders. Geier and Geier (2006) repeated this study to assess if the passing of additional time (2 years) resulted in any new diagnoses of neurodevelopmental disorders. They again concluded that thimerosal removal was correlated with a reduction in the number of neurodevelopmental disorders. Geier and Geier's report of decreased notifications of neurodevelopmental disorders to VAERS is not consistent with the CDC's (2007) account of possible increasing prevalence of autism.

A review of the literature conducted by Parker et al. (2004) found 12 studies that addressed the thimerosal-autism link, which met their inclusion criteria but varied in design and quality. Three of the studies reported previously were included in their review. Parker et al. criticized the original study conducted by Geier and Geier (2004) for its analytical approach—specifically the method of calculating prevalence. They also criticized Geier and Geier for their implication that correlation implies causation. The third study analyzed by Parker et al. was conducted by Heron and Golding (2004). The reviewers concluded that the study by Heron and Golding had both strengths and weaknesses.

The MMR vaccine has also been under suspicion as a candidate for causing autism. The Wakefield et al. (1998) controversial study implicated the MMR vaccine as a causative agent for viral encephalitis and gastrointestinal disorders such as Crohn's disease in children with neurodevelopmental disorders. The researchers suggested that an interaction could occur between viruses that affected a child's immune system, leading to gastrointestinal inflammation and permeability (also known as leaky gut) and resulted in encephalitis manifested as autism spectrum disorders. The study came under scrutiny due to flawed methodology, small sample size, and failure to provide adequate evidence to support their claims. A number of the study's authors later partially retracted the results (Murch et al., 2004).

Libbey at al. (2007) investigated the role of the MMR and diphtheria toxoid vaccine in the development of autism based on the claims that these vaccines may cause an autoimmune response that might induce autism. The researchers looked at four groups: classic onset autistic children (n = 33), regressive onset autistic children (n = 26), a neuro-typical control group (n = 25), and children with Tourette's syndrome (n = 24). No significant difference was found among the four groups for immunoglobulin.

A review by Demicheli et al. (2008) identified 139 studies relevant to the MMR-autism link, but only 31 studies met their inclusion criteria. Demicheli et al. stressed that the studies included in the review contained errors, biases, low internal and external validity, and selective reporting of results. Nonetheless, Demicheli et al. concluded that no evidence exists that points to a relationship between the MMR vaccine and autism. They highly recommended more studies of better quality.

The National Academy of Sciences' (NAS, 2004) executive summary on vaccine safety and autism has maintained that, due to the devastating nature of autism, the link between autism and vaccines cannot be casually rejected. They concur that current research has been flawed in many areas. The NAS has stressed that the significance of devastating nature of autism compels further research, but the NAS does not recommend any changes to the current immunization schedule.

Unfortunately, a growing number of parents are responding out of fear, real or not, by not vaccinating their children (CDC, 2007). Outbreaks of diseases such as measles and pertussis have been observed in scattered communities. Smith, Kennedy, Wooten, Gust, and Pickering (2006) have reported that parents who choose to not immunize usually have fears about vaccines. These same parents generally have reported that they are not influenced by their health care practitioner. Conversely, parents who are likely to vaccinate have reported that they are influenced by their health care practitioner. This behooves practitioners to build relationships with patients and families to increase vaccination rates. Additionally, families have responded positively to practitioners who respect their concerns and are willing to provide vaccines on a flexible schedule—that is, giving fewer vaccines at one visit or holding off on vaccinating if the child is ill.

Whether or not autism is actually increasing is not easily answered. A faction largely comprised of parents and health care professionals with autistic children question the safety of vaccines. Unfortunately, research to date has been overwhelmingly flawed and biased on both sides of the argument. The CDC and the NAS both encourage further research concerning autism but both agencies, as do most leading government agencies, reject a causal relationship of vaccines and autism. Before rejecting the link between autism and vaccines, evidence must be produced that expands on the current state of knowledge. It is worth considering, however, that if leading government agencies are rejecting the vaccine-autism link, then researchers may have a difficult time obtaining funding to conduct appropriate studies. The public health benefit of vaccines has been recognized for years, but since the memory of infectious disease outbreaks has faded (most people haven't experienced a significant outbreak), parents are questioning the wisdom of vaccines. It's left to health care providers, then, to help parents make sense of the most current information and to help parents make decisions that are best for the child but also for society.

References

Autism Research Institute. (2002). The autism-vaccine disaster. *Autism Research Review International,16*(3), 3.

Autism Research Institute. (2005). Treatment options for mercury/metal toxicity in autism and related neurodevelopmental disorders: Consensus position paper. Retrieved from www.autismresearchinstitute.com

Autism Research Institute. (2008). *About us.* Retrieved from www.autismresearchinstitute.com

Baker, J. (2008). Mercury, vaccines, and autism: One controversy, three histories. *American Journal of Public Health, 98*(2), 244–253.

Centers for Disease Control. (2007). Autism information center. Retrieved from www.cdc.gov/ncbddd/autism/

Demicheli, V., Jefferson, T., Rivetti, A., & Price, D. (2008). Vaccines for measles, mumps, and rubella in children (review). *The Cochrane Collaboration* (1–36). New York: Wiley.

Geier, D. A., & Geier, M. R. (2004). Neurodevelopmental disorders following thimerosal-containing childhood immunizations: A follow-up analysis. *International Journal of Toxicology, 23*(6), 369–376.

Geier, D. A., & Geier, M. R. (2006). An assessment of downward trends in neurodevelopmental disorders in the United States following removal of thimerosal from childhood vaccines. *Medical Science Monitor, 12*(6), 231–239.

Heron, J., & Golding, J. (2004). Thimerosal exposure in infants and developmental disorders: A prospective cohort study in the United Kingdom does not support a causal association. *Pediatrics, 114,* 577–583.

Libbey, J. E., Coon, H. H., Kirkman, N. J., Sweeten, T. L., Miller, J. N., Lainhart, J. E., et al. (2007). Are there altered antibody responses to measles, mumps, and rubella viruses in autism? *Journal of Neurovirology, 13,* 252–259.

Murch, S. H., Anthony, A., Casson, D. H., Malik, M., Berelowitz, M., Dhillon, A.P., et al. (2004). Retraction of an interpretation. *The Lancet 363*(9411), 750.

National Academy of Sciences. (2004). Immunization safety review: Vaccines and autism. Executive Summary. Retrieved from www.nap.edu

Parker, S. K., Schwartz, B., Todd, J., & Pickering, L. K. (2004). Thimerosal-containing vaccines and autism spectrum disorder: A critical review of published original data. *Pediatrics, 114,* 793–804.

Schechter, R., & Grether, J. K. (2008). Continuing increases in autism reported to California's developmental services system. *Archives of General Psychiatry, 65*(1), 19–24.

Smith, P.M., Kennedy, A.M., Wooten, K., Gust, D.A., & Pickering, L.K. (2006). Association between health care providers' influence on parents who have concerns about vaccine safety and vaccination coverage. *Pediatrics 118*(5), 1287–1292.

Taylor, B. (2006). Vaccines and the changing epidemiology of autism. *The Author Journal Compilation, 32*(5), 511–519.

Thompson, W.W., Price, C., Goodson, B., Shay, D. K., Benson, P., Hinrichsen, V. L., et al. (2007). Early thimerosal exposure and neuropsychological outcomes at 7 to 10 years. *The New England Journal of Medicine, 357*(13), 1281–1292.

Wakefield, A. J., Murch, S. H., Anthony, A., Linell, J., Casson, D. M., Malik, M., et al. (1998). Ileal-lymphoid-nodular hyperplasia, non-specific colitis, and pervasive developmental disorder in children. *The Lancet, 351*, 637–641.

From: The Michigan Corpus of Upper-level Student Papers (MICUSP).

Strategy: Listening for and Making Educated Guesses

When researchers present their results or lecturers discuss others' results, they may not be absolutely certain of their words. One way speakers can avoid stating certainties is by hedging. Review the information in Unit 4 on page 65. Another way speakers can alert the listeners that they are simply making an educated guess is to use certain signal phrases.

I'd say that . . . .

It [certainly] looks like . . . .

It seems to be . . . .

Although it's difficult to say for sure, the results indicate . . . .

I strongly believe that . . . .

It seems to be almost conclusive . . . .

With little doubt . . . .

I'd venture to say . . . .

The results lean heavily in favor of/against . . . .

I definitely think there are . . . .

Practice Activity: Making Educated Guesses

Answer these questions from the reading. Try not to look back at the reading. If you're not sure of your answer, use phrasing to indicate that you are making an educated guess.

1. What is the hypothesis regarding the connection between vaccinations and autism?

   _____

2. In the review of the research presented, what are the findings?

   _____

   _____

   _____

3. How conclusive are the results? What language is used that shows the author's level of certainty about the researchers discussed in the article?

   _____

   _____

   _____

4. What are the potential problems of not immunizing children?

   _____

   _____

   _____

5. What can health-care providers do to mitigate these concerns?

   _____

   _____

   _____

Speaking

Presenting an Argument or Drawing Attention to a Strong Belief

Academic discussions and presentations often contain arguments. These arguments may be about issues, data, or ideas. Good speakers strengthen a point they want the listener to notice by using certain words or phrases. Using these phrases can be very persuasive or alert listeners that the speaker is trying to convince them of something. Speakers may use these phrases in conjunction with boosting (pages 78–79).

> The real question is . . .
>
> I think we need to focus on one thing . . .
>
> You can't ignore . . .
>
> What I'm trying to say is . . .
>
> The data we need to look at is . . .
>
> You can't argue the fact that . . .
>
> What's most important is . . .
>
> You must agree that . . .
>
> You'll see . . .
>
> Take X, for example, . . .
>
> I definitely think . . . .
>
> If you look at it this way . . . .

Practice Activity: Presenting an Argument

Write a few notes to help you answer the questions. Then discuss them with a partner. Agree and disagree with each other and draw attention to the points you think are most important by using appropriate phrases.

1. Does age affect how well you can learn a second language?

_____

_____

_____

2. What civilization has influenced the modern world the most?

_____

_____

_____

3. What natural disaster has affected the most people?

_____

_____

_____

4. Why should people support microloans in poor communities?

_____

_____

_____

5. What can people do preventively to promote good health?

_____

_____

_____

Listening 2: Recognizing Strong Beliefs and Points of View

Listening in Groups (Video)

Listen to the students expess their beliefs about values and ethics. Discuss these questions in a small group.

Focus on Language

1. How strongly do the speakers feel? What language do they use to help express their feelings?

   _____

   _____

2. What phrases are used to express agreement? (<u>Note</u>: Don't worry about writing the exact words.)

   _____

   _____

3. What phrases are used to express disagreement? (<u>Note</u>: Don't worry about writing the exact words.)

   _____

   _____

Focus on Tone

1. The word *interesting* is used after the first three opinions are expressed. What does the tone indicate about the person's level of agreement to the opinion it follows? Why do you think the word *interesting* is used so frequently during this interaction?

   _____

   _____

2. The last speaker talks about absolute morals. How strongly do you think he feels? What clues does his voice give?

   _____

   _____

Focus on Nonverbal Communication

1. What nonverbal cues are used to show agreement?

   _____

   _____

2. What nonverbal cues are used to show disagreement?

   _____

   _____

3. What nonverbal cue emphasizes the word *justify?*

   _____

   _____

4. One student says, *Right* at the end. The word is typically used to show agreement. Do you believe her agreement is genuine? Why or why not?

   _____

   _____

Summary

1. At the end, on what point do the four students agree?

   _____

   _____

2. Which student would you most like to work with? Why?

   _____

   _____

Part 3: Causes of Communication Difficulties

Getting Started

A variety of disorders can lead to speech and hearing impairments. There are some methods that can be implemented to help people communicate despite their impairments. For example, sign language is a tool in which people can communicate messages after having lost their hearing. Answer these questions with a partner.

1. What do you think are possible causes for speech loss? What means have you observed people using to augment their speech?

2. What experiences have you had communicating with a person using any kind of assistive technology to communicate (anything from pen and paper to electronic devices) even when there are no physical impairments?

3. From your experience, how are people with speech or hearing impairments supported in schools or at work?

Strategy: Managing Open Lecture Style

Many lecturers will use a more informal, open lecture style that can sometimes make identifying the important points difficult. Despite that, many students find a lecturer using an open style is more interesting. They prefer this to listening to a long lecture full of facts that is delivered without more spontaneous comments or digressions or they prefer active body language from the speaker.

An open-style lecturer tends to:

- ask direct questions
- digress; tell stories
- direct focus back to the content when necessary
- be more animated in movements while lecturing
- involve students in the delivery of content.

Also note that an open lecture style includes participation from the listeners, including answering questions and seeking clarification.

Open lecturers, because of their style, tend to use certain phrases.

Inviting participation with direct questions followed by a pause

What different things can go wrong with . . . ?

Any other places . . . ?

Have you read about . . . ?

Everyone knows what it is, don't you?

What does it mean to . . . .?

Okay, so what about . . . .?

Student requests for clarification, opinions, or other input

Is _____ the _____one?

So what are/is _____?

I have a question [about that last slide].

Digressions/personal anecdotes

It's actually kind of interesting. When I . . . .

By the way, [there's a fascinating] . . . .

I met someone at one of my professional conferences who . . . .

Let's back up.

That reminds me.

There's a story here.

Getting back on topic

But let's get back to . . . .

As I was saying before we got off track . . . .

Okay, now then . . . .

I want to return to . . . .

There are some nonverbal cues as well. Open-style lecturers will likely be standing or moving around and will not usually sit or stand at a lectern. They often take a drink of their water before getting back on topic or have to move through several slides or visual aids quickly to "match" where their digression or student question has led them.

Practice Activity: Being an Open-Style Speaker

Read this information from the National Institute of Health about aphasia. Form a small group and divide the reading into parts. Imagine you are an open-style speaker who has to present this information. Add a direct question, words and phrases, and a digression to your part. When you are finished, read your section to your group and be prepared for them to ask questions as you deliver your lecture.

What Is Aphasia?

Aphasia is a disorder that results from damage to portions of the brain that are responsible for language. For most people, these are areas on the left side (hemisphere) of the brain. Aphasia usually occurs suddenly, often as the result of a stroke or head injury, but it may also develop slowly, as in the case of a brain tumor, an infection, or dementia. The disorder impairs the expression and understanding of language as well as reading and writing. Aphasia may co-occur with speech disorders such as dysarthria or apraxia of speech, which also result from brain damage.

Who Has Aphasia?

Anyone can acquire aphasia, including children, but most people who have aphasia are middle-aged or older. Men and women are equally affected. According to the National Aphasia Association, approximately 80,000 individuals acquire aphasia each year from strokes. About one million people in the United States currently have aphasia.

What Causes Aphasia?

Aphasia is caused by damage to one or more of the language areas of the brain. Many times, the cause of the brain injury is a stroke. A stroke occurs when blood is unable to reach a part of the brain. Brain cells die when they do not receive their normal supply of blood, which carries oxygen and important nutrients. Other causes of brain injury are severe blows to the head, brain tumors, brain infections, and other conditions that affect the brain.

How Is Aphasia Diagnosed?

Aphasia is usually first recognized by the physician who treats the person for his or her brain injury. Frequently this is a neurologist. The physician typically performs tests that require the person to follow commands, answer questions, name objects, and carry on a conversation. If the physician suspects aphasia, the patient is often referred to a speech-language pathologist, who performs a comprehensive examination of the person's communication abilities. The examination includes the person's ability to speak, express ideas, converse socially, understand language, read, and write, as well as the ability to swallow and to use alternative and augmentative communication.

How Is Aphasia Treated?

In some cases, a person will completely recover from aphasia without treatment. This type of spontaneous recovery usually occurs following a type of stroke in which blood flow to the brain is temporarily interrupted but quickly restored, called a transient ischemic attack. In these circumstances, language abilities may return in a few hours or a few days.

For most cases, however, language recovery is not as quick or as complete. While many people with aphasia experience partial spontaneous recovery, in which some language abilities return a few days to a month after the brain injury, some amount of aphasia typically remains. In these instances, speech-language therapy is often helpful. Recovery usually continues over a two-year period. Many health professionals believe that the most effective treatment begins early in the recovery process. Some of the factors that influence the amount of improvement include the cause of the brain damage, the area of the brain that was damaged, the extent of the brain injury, and the age and health of the individual. Additional factors include motivation, handedness, and educational level.

Aphasia therapy aims to improve a person's ability to communicate by helping him or her to use remaining language abilities, restore language abilities as much as possible, compensate for language problems, and learn other methods of communicating. Individual therapy focuses on the specific needs of the person, while group therapy offers the opportunity to use new communication skills in a small-group setting. Stroke clubs, regional support groups formed by people who have had a stroke, are available in most major cities. These clubs also offer the opportunity for people with aphasia to try new communication skills. In addition, stroke clubs can help a person and his or her family adjust to the life changes that accompany stroke and aphasia. Family involvement is often a crucial component of aphasia treatment so that family members can learn the best way to communicate with their loved one.

Family members are encouraged to:

- Simplify language by using short, uncomplicated sentences.
- Repeat the content words or write down key words to clarify meaning as needed.
- Maintain a natural conversational manner appropriate for an adult.
- Minimize distractions, such as a loud radio or TV, whenever possible.
- Include the person with aphasia in conversations.
- Ask for and value the opinion of the person with aphasia, especially regarding family matters.
- Encourage any type of communication, whether it is speech, gesture, pointing, or drawing.
- Avoid correcting the person's speech.
- Allow the person plenty of time to talk.
- Help the person become involved outside the home. Seek out support groups such as stroke clubs.

Other treatment approaches involve the use of computers to improve the language abilities of people with aphasia. Studies have shown that computer-assisted therapy can help people with aphasia retrieve certain parts of speech, such as the use of verbs. Computers can also provide an alternative system of communication for people with difficulty expressing language. Lastly, computers can help people who have problems perceiving the difference between phonemes (the sounds from which words are formed) by providing auditory discrimination exercises.

From: National Institute on Deafness and Other Communication Disorders, National Institutes of Health. *Aphasia*. 2010. www.nidcd.nih.gov/health/voice/pages/aphasia.aspx.

Research Strategy: Primary Research in Depth

Primary research, as discussed in Unit 4, consists of data from "original" sources such as interviews or surveys.

Interviews may be with experts in the field or with subjects who have experienced (or are experiencing) the topic you are writing about. For example, if you were to write about aphasia, you may interview a doctor about the treatments. Although your topic helps determine how many interviews you will conduct, many papers have only a few interviewees, but the interviews are very detailed and in-depth. You will have to prepare many strong, open-ended questions in advance.

Surveys are collections of questions. You may only talk to a person for a couple of minutes, but you'll ask them a series of questions that help you collect data. Sometimes you might present questions in writing that people will respond to in writing. These questions aren't as in-depth. In other words, you may have only short, yes-no questions or questions that ask someone to rank priorities or say if they like or dislike something. Because the questions are quick and surveys don't take as much time, you are more likely to conduct many of them in order to generate enough data from which to draw conclusions. For example, if you want to find out how many people know sign language, you can't just ask one person. That would not give you a representative sample. However, if you ask 50 people, and learn that 5 know sign language, then you can draw a conclusion that 10 percent of the people know sign language. The more surveys you have, the more reliable the results.

Practice Activity: Designing Primary Research

Think about your own field of interest. What would you like to learn more about? Answer these questions.

Topic: _____

1. Who would you interview?

2. What are three questions you would ask that person?

3. Who would you survey? Where would you conduct your survey? Approximately how many people would you try to survey?

4. What are 10 questions you would ask your subjects?

Vocabulary Power

There are a number of terms and phrases in this lecture that you may encounter in other academic settings. Add at least five vocabulary items to your vocabulary notebook or log.
    Match the words in bold with a definition on the right.

_____ 1. What kinds of speech **impairments** would these different conditions cause?

_____ 2. Let's look at the definition of augmentative and alternative communication, which we will **henceforth** call AAC.

_____ 3. We want to **augment** the person's— well, whatever ability he or she has for communicating.

_____ 4. However, to really be effective, you often want to, use a **multimodal** communication that combines different aspects.

_____ 5. Now, the advent of email has **blurred** that somewhat in that we treat email as a conversation, and tend to ignore all the formal rules of writing.

_____ 6. . . . if I didn't have motor control, a lot would get lost. How do you **compensate** for that?

_____ 7. You have to have a control **interface** that the person can operate efficiently . . . .

_____ 8. Sometimes a person's communication system will just be a microphone and **amplifier.**

a. something that increases sound

b. damage

c. having several forms

d. make up for

e. made difficult to see

f. from this point forward

g. something that allows two elements to communicate

h. improve

Listening 3: Aphasia and Assistive Technology and Communication

Listening to a Lecture

Listen to the lecture. Take notes on a separate sheet of paper. What features of an open-style lecture do you hear?

Checking Your Understanding: Main Ideas

Review your notes. Listen again to the lecture if necessary. Put a check mark (✓) next to the statements that best reflect the main ideas of the lecture.

_____ People with speech disorders have some form of aphasia and will have trouble both understanding and producing speech.

_____ People with aphasia communicate using American Sign Language.

_____ The choice of communicative devices is highly dependent on each individual's needs and circumstances.

_____ There is more than one type of aphasia.

Panel Discussion

In the United States, individuals with physical and cognitive disabilities are protected under the Americans with Disabilities Act (ADA). The ADA prohibits employers from discriminating against qualified individuals with disabilities in job hiring, firing, advancement, compensation, training, or other employment benefits. A qualified person is one with proper education, experiences, and skills. A person with a disability is defined as anyone with a physical or mental impairment that significantly limits life activities. A qualified employee or applicant with a disability is someone who can perform the essential functions of the job, with or without reasonable accommodation. Reasonable accommodation may include making facilities accessible to and usable by those with disabilities; modifying work schedules; modifying equipment or devices; adjusting or modifying examinations, training materials, or policies; and providing qualified interpreters. Universities must also adhere to these practices with incoming and current students.

There are many countries around the world where these same protections are not provided due to attitudes and limited resources. Some argue that it should be the government who pays for accommodations, not companies or businesses themselves. In teams of three, do some light research on existing guidelines that protect individuals with disabilities.

Each panelist will do research on the chosen topic and present as if he/she were an expert in this topic. The panelists may have opposing views or may present as a team. Each panelist should speak for at least five minutes. Afterward, the rest of the class will ask the panelists questions.

Topic: _____

Team member responsibilities (which aspects of the topic is each going to research):

_____

_____

_____

_____

_____

_____

Questions for other panelists:

_____

_____

_____

_____

_____

_____

Rapid Vocabulary Review

From the three answers on the right, circle the one that best explains the vocabulary item on the left as it is used in this unit.

Vocabulary	Answers		
Synonyms			
flow	difference	movement	pressure
device	person	place	thing
onset	beginning	termination	source
intelligible	between	silent	coherent
flawed	imperfect	illegal	irrelevant
adhere	stick	drive	bake
compel	prohibit	force	request
burgeoning	linking	growing	reporting
prevalence	coordination	commonness	likelihood
modify	change	agree	qualify
Combinations and Associations			
paint a _____	drawing	picture	sketch
on the flip _____	part	corner	side
a short _____ of time	window	door	path
a substantial _____	first	increase	country
wrap _____	in	on	up
comprised _____	at	of	in
a causal _____	friendship	relationship	family
_____ scrutiny	between	against	under
to a _____ degree	clear	certain	practice
_____ some point	on	in	at

⇨✕⊐ Synthesizing: Projects and Presentations

Short In-Class Assignments	Longer Outside Assignments
What Do the Numbers Mean?	**Research Findings Report**
Use a copy of the school or local newspaper and find a chart or graph with statistics. With a partner, write a script discussing the statistics, talking about the topic, presenting ideas, and making educated guesses. Then show your chart or graph to another pair (or to the class) and perform your script.	Choose two research articles related to one of the following topics: • Causes of a neurological problem (your choice) • Devices for assisting people with a neurological disorder As you read your studies, pay attention to the language used to report the findings. Include data in your report. How conclusive are they? How sound were the studies? Prepare a report and presentation of what you read and be ready to report to your classmates. Include visual aids. Use appropriate language to present your arguments, talk about statistics, and make educated guesses.
My Proposal	**Conducting Primary Research**
Write a topic of interest that you'd like to talk more about. These may come from the school or local newspaper, current events, university activities, class projects, or any other general topic(s). Collect the topics in a bag. When it is your turn, pull a card from the bag. Read the topic and propose to the class why this is a topic worth discussing in more detail.	Choose an expert in your field to interview or prepare a survey to give to 20 people. Write the questions, conduct the interview/survey, collect the data, and provide results using your survey. Prepare a presentation to discuss your experience and your results. Include visual aids to enhance your presentation.

Vocabulary Log

To increase your vocabulary knowledge, write a definition or translation for each vocabulary item. Then write an original phrase, sentence, or note that will help you remember the vocabulary item.

Vocabulary Item	Definition or Translation	Your Original Phrase, Sentence, or Note
1. infections		
2. sophisticated		
3. outbreak		
4. incidence		
5. transient		
6. augmentative		
7. alternative		
8. diagnosis		
9. controversial		
10. receptive		
11. spontaneous		
12. mission		
13. expressive		

Vocabulary Item	Definition or Translation	Your Original Phrase, Sentence, or Note
14. correlate		
15. auditory		
16. efficient		
17. continuum		
18. ignore		
19. dysfunction		
20. adequate		
21. disorder		
22. wander		
23. deficit		
24. enhancement		
25. encompass		

Engineering: Management Science

Management science is a discipline that studies the tools and methods used to make decisions and solve problems. Since it requires statistics, technology, and modeling to determine the best decision or solution, it is often found housed within the field of engineering. Those with degrees in Management Science might also be involved in developing policies, designing engineering systems, and analyzing organizational structures for businesses, entrepreneurial efforts, government organizations, or academic institutions. This unit considers management science and various aspects of engineering.

Part 1: Problem Solving

Getting Started

All disciplines require problem solving in some form, some to larger degrees than others. One goal of problem solving is to find an ideal and achievable solution with specific and clear objectives. Some scientists solve a problem with a product, system, or process. Many strategies are used to try to solve problems, such as brainstorming, testing, analyzing, trial-and-error, and researching. When a solution is found, it is often explained in a formal presentation or written in a publication. Review problem-and-solution language on page 62. Answer these questions with a partner.

1. President Lyndon B. Johnson once said, "There are no problems we cannot solve together, and very few we can solve by ourselves." What kinds of problems can you think of that benefit from having more than one person involved? Are there any problems that are better worked on independently?

2. Discuss a problem you need to solve. Consider academic problems, such as a math problem or experiment or another type of problem such as balancing study time with leisure time. Brainstorm possible solutions to this problem. Can you choose the best solution from your list?

Strategy: Listening to Short Pitches (or Elevator Speeches)

Once a problem has been solved, the problem, solution, and the research conducted are often explained in an oral presentation or in a publication. One goal is to present the ideas in a way that the audience members, who may not be experts in the field, can understand in a short amount of time. One version of this is called the elevator pitch or elevator speech. An elevator pitch is a summary of your idea that is interesting, comprehensible, and short. The idea is that you can deliver your speech in the time it takes to ride in an elevator. One common elevator speech is one in which a person sells him or herself to a prospective employer. An academic version of this is the three-minute thesis competition (3MT™). In the competition, graduate and postgraduate students have an opportunity to present their research and its significance to a nonspecialist audience and have to do it in only three minutes. A good elevator pitch or three-minute thesis will include many of the strategies studied in Units 1–5 of this textbook. Take a few minutes to review the strategies.

Practice Activity: Identifying a Speaker's Skills

Read this text from a winning three-minute thesis. Which strategies from Units 1–5 can you find?

When I was little, I didn't like going to the the doctor at all 'cause it usually meant something awful like a needle or a throat swab. I always thought it would be great if doctors had a little gadget that they could just scan you with and then up on the screen would pop the diagnosis. Unfortunately, though, something like that still only exists in science fiction.

But we are taking our first step towards one. You see, researchers have been working on something called a breath analyzer, and it works like an electronic nose, sniffing out human breath for the presence of certain molecules. And that's important because medical researchers have discovered that specific combinations of molecules in human breath corresponds to diseases like cancer, Parkinson's, Alzheimer's, and more. Wouldn't it be great if diagnosis of these diseases were as simple as breathing into a tube? So what's the hold up? Why don't we have a breath analyzer today?

Well, the tricky part has been finding a sensor that can detect these molecules but that's also compact and cheap so that we can have our little handheld device in every doctor's office. Well, one solution to that problem is the nanocantilever. Now, nanocantilevers are like tiny little diving boards, so they're attached at one end and free to move at the other. But they're really tiny...about a hundred times smaller than a human hair, in fact. And since they're so small, just the weight of a single molecule on the end of that nanocantilever is enough to make it bend. So if we had hundreds of these nanocantilevers and coated each of them with a compound that different types of molecules like to stick to, then we could detect these different diseases in human breath all at once. So, for example, maybe if Cantilevers 1 and 3 were triggered, that might mean that the patient has Alzheimer's.

So, now, cantilevers seem to be just about perfect. But there is one catch. Since the nanocantilevers are so tiny and they're not moving very much at all, it's extremely difficult to measure how much they bend. And that's where my research comes in. I've been working on a new technique for measuring how much nanocantilevers bend. So what I do is I fabricate nanocantilevers right here on campus. And I figured out a way to attach an extremely thin gold wire to one edge of that nanocantilever and the other end is fixed. So as that nanocantilever bends, that really thin gold wire stretches, and we can measure that electrically. And that is how we can read out extremely tiny motions of these little cantilever beams. Now this technology is still brand new, so I wouldn't expect to see a nanocantilever-powered breath analyzer on the market any time soon. But don't be surprised if one day you walk into your doctor's office and there's no prickly needles, there's no scratchy throat swabs. Instead, all they ask you to do is breathe into a tube. Thank you.

From: Queen's University, School of Graduate Studies Three Minute Thesis Competition, April 30th, 2012; Nanocantilevers: A New Tool for Medical Diagnostics; Jennifer Campbell, Engineering Physics, Ph.D. candidate; Supervisor: Dr. Robert Knobel: http://threeminutethesis.org/3mt-showcase. Used with permission.

Speaking

Being Compelling and Persuasive

The 3MT™ was started at The University of Queensland and is now held at universities around the world. Not only do students have the chance to present their research, but they also have the opportunity to practice their speaking and presenting skills. Students in the competition are judged in three categories: comprehension, engagement, and communication. Some of the criteria that have been used to judge some of the 3MT™ competitions are listed (www.uq.edu.au/grad-school/3mt).

COMPREHENSION

- Did the presentation help the audience understand the research?
- Did the presenter clearly outline the nature and aims of the research?
- Do you know what is significant about this research?
- Did the presentation follow a logical sequence?

ENGAGEMENT

- Did the oration make the audience want to know more?
- Was the presenter careful not to trivialize or dumb down his/her research?
- Did the presenter convey enthusiasm for his/her work?
- Did the presenter capture and maintain the audience's attention?
- Would I like to know more about the speaker's research?

COMMUNICATION

- Was the thesis topic and its significance communicated in language appropriate to a non-specialist audience?
- Did the speaker use sufficient eye contact and vocal range and maintain a steady pace and a confident stance?
- Did the speaker avoid scientific jargon, explain terminology that needed to be used, and provide adequate background information to illustrate points?
- Did the presenter spend the right amount of time on each element of the presentation—or did he or she elaborate for too long or seem rushed?
- Did the PowerPoint slide enhance, rather than detract from, the presentation—was it clear, legible, and concise?

Practice Activity: Thinking about Your Own Strengths and Weaknesses

Review the judging criteria in the box on page 157. Choose a speech or presentation you gave in Units 1–5 of this textbook. Answer the questions about your own speech. Then answer these questions.

1. Which category, comprehension, engagement, or communication, do you feel is your strongest? Why do you think you are strong in that category?

   _____

   _____

2. Which category do you feel is your weakest? What can you do to improve that category?

   _____

   _____

Listening 1: Listening to a 3MT™

Listening to a Student Presentation

Go to one of the online sites featuring 3MTs™ (threeminutethesis.org), and select one presentation to listen to. Then answer these questions.

Title: _____

1. Which strategies listed on page 157 do you think the speaker used most effectively?

   _____

   _____

   _____

2. Are there any strategies that you felt could have been used more effectively? Why or why not?

   _____

   _____

   _____

3. Using the judging criteria (see page 157), how many questions would you answer yes to? For any no answers, what could the speaker do to change your mind?

_____

_____

_____

4. Using the judging criteria, what category do you feel is the speaker's strongest?

_____

_____

_____

Making an Impromptu Speech

You will have three minutes to give an impromptu speech that mirrors an elevator speech convincing a hiring manager that you are the best person for the job you want to have when you finish school.

Part 2: Sustainability

Getting Started

Sustainability is concept that a resource is used in such a way that it is not completely depleted or damaged. With discussions of some of the world's resources being depleted, such as oil, solutions for sustaining the current resources or finding a new resource to replace it are necessary. Engineering is just one field that is concerned about sustainability. Answer these questions with a partner.

1. Can you think of any resources that have already been depleted? How did this impact society?

2. What resources can you name that are not sustainable? What will the impact be on society if this resource is depleted? Can you think of a replacement or another solution?

Sustainability is a hot topic in many fields, but especially in Engineering courrses. This unit's reading is from a textbook in an Engineering or Policy course.

Reading
Reading about Innovation

Engineers and Sustainable Development
(1980s to the Present)

Sustainable development was a trend that developed largely out of the failures of the development strategies of the 1970s and 1980s. One of the key events in this history was the 1992 United Nations Conference on Environment and Development in Rio de Janeiro (also known as the Earth Summit), out of which came the Rio Declaration.

We have identified two dominant views of sustainable development—the weak and the strong (Neumayer, E., 1999). *Weak sustainability*, also called "constrained growth," emphasizes economic models that do not differentiate between natural and human-made resources. Proponents of this view assume that scientific and technological advancement will address natural resource depletion and emphasize the importance of economic and social gains in the face of environmental degradation. Due to its reliance on technological solutions, most engineers have traditionally supported this approach (see Figure 6.1).

Proponents of *strong sustainability* acknowledge that natural resources cannot always be treated like human-made resources because of natural constraints such as irreversibility of ecological damage—for example, you cannot bring an animal species back to life once it is gone. This view argues for the protection of natural resources even at the cost of development opportunities—and an example of that is saving the spotted owl even if it means losing growth opportunities for the timber industry.

Lacking the nationalistic luster of economic competitiveness, which placed engineers at the center stage of technological innovation in the 1980s, sustainable development was only a marginal preoccupation for engineers in the 1990s. Among a myriad of reports linking technological development to economic competitiveness, one on *Technology and Environment*, by the U.S. National Academy of Engineering (NAE), called for "[engineers as] creators of new technological developments and policymakers...to develop guidelines and policies for sustainable development that

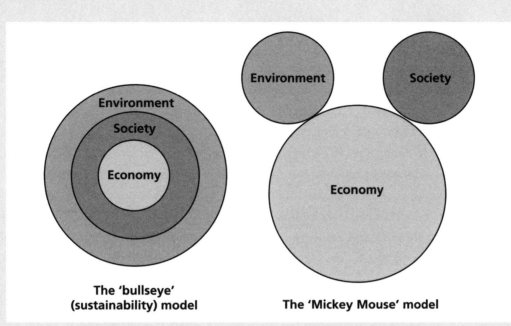

Figure 6.1: Strong sustainability can be depicted with the economy as dependent on social and economic activity which in turn are dependent of the natural environment. Activities that are harmful to the environment damage both society and the economy (the "bullseye" model). Weak sustainability can be represented with the economy as the main focus of human activity and both society and the environment as relevant but tangential considerations. In the 'Mickey Mouse' model, protecting the environment might be desirable but not essential to society or the economy. Source: http://www.ozpolitic.com/articles/environment-society-economy.html. Used with permission.

reflect for the long-term, global implications of large-scale technologies and that support the innovation of less intrusive, more adaptable technologies at all levels" (Ausubel and Sladovich, 1989).

Despite such calls, sustainable development did not provide the market demand that would justify investments in new sustainable technologies. By contrast, economic competitiveness clearly challenged engineers to develop technologies for ever growing international markets. Most corporate employers of U.S. engineers were simply not willing to take sustainable technology investment risks. New markets for sustainable technologies had to be created with government incentives and through policy decisions such as those highlighted by President Clinton's Council on Sustainable Development (1993–96) (Zwally, 1996). Unfortunately, neither the Clinton nor the Bush administrations provided sufficient incentives to create these markets. It remains to be seen whether the commitment of the Obama administration toward renewable energy materializes in such markets, products, and jobs—which could attract future generations of engineers.

KEY TERMS

Weak sustainability: This conception of sustainability sees natural resources much the way we see economic ones—as something to be priced, bought, sold, and managed. It views nature in terms of markets, economic worth, and technocratic management. Its appeal is that it does little to challenge prevailing beliefs about economic growth and human consumption, assuming that natural resources can simply be incorporated into existing economic models. Its disadvantage is that it doesn't take into account important characteristics that make natural resources different from human-produced resources such as their finite nature and our utter dependence on them for survival. The cap and trade approach to CO_2 emissions is an example of weak sustainability.

Strong sustainability: This model assumes that environmental or natural resources have intrinsic value in relation to other forms of capital and human-made resources. While pollution is often "externalized" in the weak model, it would be accounted for in the strong model because it represents damaging of natural capital, or the commons. The advantage of this model is that it makes good ecological sense; we cannot have a timber industry, for example, if there are no trees to harvest due to over-logging. On the other hand, it has proven very difficult to change the economic system to include "externalities" because the weak model is so in line with our deeply ingrained assumptions about what has worth.

In engineering education, sustainable development did not become a major theme in the 1990s, marginally appearing through the concerns of a small community of activist engineering educators that annually puts together the International Symposium on Technology and Society (ISTAS) of the Institute of Electrical and Electronics Engineers (IEEE). In 1991, ISTAS held a symposium entitled "Preparing for a Sustainable Society." Sustainable development became a theme around which a handful of engineering educators proposed new curricula in engineering ethics, economics and the academic field known as science, technology, and society (STS) (IEEE, 1991). Unfortunately, at that time, these proposals became secondary in engineering programs, largely because economic competitiveness was challenging most engineering faculty to focus curricular development in areas that U.S. engineering students seemed to be lacking, such as design, manufacturing, and international education. The calls for "flexible engineers" that would help the U.S. compete in a global economy did not include competencies related to sustainable development (Lucena, J., 2003).

Engineers Heed the Call to Sustainable Development (Late 1990s-Present)

In contrast to the preceding decades, engineering organizations in the early 21st century heeded the call to sustainable development and have begun taking actions, ranging from hosting regional and world conferences to declaring their position with respect to sustainable development, to revising their codes of ethics and challenging members to address sustainable development principles in their work, and creating international professional partnerships such as the World Engineering Partnership for Sustainable Development (WEPSD). The WEPSD vision statement indicates that:

> Engineers will translate the dreams of humanity, traditional knowledge, and the concepts of science into action through the creative application of technology to achieve sustainable development. The ethics, education, and practices of the engineering profession will shape a sustainable future for all generations. To achieve this vision, the leadership of the world engineering community will join together in an integrated partnership to actively engage with all disciplines and decision makers to provide advice, leadership, and facilitation for our shared and sustainable world. (World Federation of Engineering Organizations, 1997, 7)

In 1999, the American Society of Engineering Education (ASEE) released a "Statement on Sustainable Development Education" which states that Engineering students should learn about sustainable development and sustainability in the general education component of the curriculum as they are preparing for the major design experience. For example, studies of economics and ethics are necessary to understand the need to use sustainable engineering techniques, including improved clean technologies. In teaching sustainable design, faculty should ask their students to consider the impacts of design upon U.S. society, and upon other nations and cultures. Engineering faculty should use systems approaches, including interdisciplinary teams, to teach pollution prevention techniques, life cycle analysis, industrial ecology, and other sustainable engineering concepts. . . . ASEE believes that engineering graduates must be prepared by their education to use sustainable engineering techniques in the practice of their profession and to take leadership roles in facilitating sustainable development in their communities" (ASEE Board of Directors, 1999).

In addition, as a part of its code of ethics, the American Society of Civil Engineers (ASCE) has declared that its engineers shall "strive to comply with the principles of sustainable development," which is defined as "the challenge of meeting human needs for natural resources, industrial products, energy, food, transportation, shelter, and effective waste management while conserving and protecting environmental quality and the natural resource base essential for future development." Other professional societies and organizations have followed suit.

Although sustainable development did not challenge engineers to compete in the international arena in the same way that economic competitiveness has done since the 1990s, it became an interesting problem for some engineers to solve through a systems approach. Some engineers appropriated "sustainable development" as an effort to be achieved through the use of technologies to clean up the mess that previous industrial practices had created and positioned themselves as "central players" in the success or failure of this effort (Prendergast, 1993). Ironically, the systems approach that emerged in the 1950s out of military technological development (Hughes et al., 2000) was favored again as a key engineering tool to solve the challenges of sustainable development. This systems approach to sustainability has become institutionalized in a small number of engineering education programs such as University of Michigan's Engineering Sustainable Systems dual-degree. Figure 6.2 is an example of a systems approach to modeling a lake that reveals the complexity of the relationship among biophysical and socio-economic parameters.

This is a welcome improvement in engineers' understanding of how human systems interact with ecological ones. Yet excessive analysis of these interactions can lead to inaction. In his excellent summary of systems approaches to sustainability, including those developed by engineers and other scientists, Joseph Fiksel, in 2006, warned us that "[w]hile improving modeling techniques and establishing a rigorous science of sustainability is important, a caveat is in order. Excessive modeling efforts may become an excuse for delaying effective political action, leading to 'paralysis by analysis'.... Progress in theory-based research needs to be balanced with exploratory policy implementation that will enrich our understanding of sustainability issues in real-world systems."

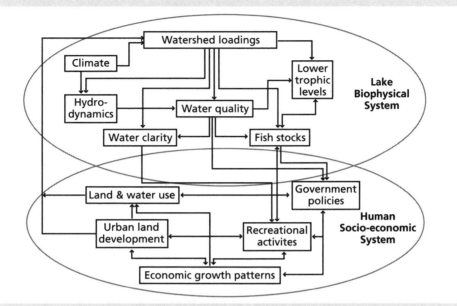

Figure 6.2: *Modeling of Coupled Parameters*
in a Lake System (Fiksel, 2006)

As the end of the 20th century approached, some engineering educators incorporated sustainable development in the desired set of knowledge and skills for the engineer of the 21st century (Velazquez et al., 1999). The emergence of new ABET accreditation criteria for engineering programs in the U.S. in 2000 facilitated this adoption, especially the criterion that calls for engineering graduates to have "an ability to design a system, component, or process to meet desired needs within realistic constraints such as economic, environmental, social, political, ethical, health and safety, manufacturability, and sustainability." Furthermore, the influential *Engineer of 2020* report by the National Academy of Engineering challenged engineers in the 21st century to adopt the tools for sustainable designs to the local conditions of developing countries in order to ensure equity in the benefits from using these tools across the world (National Academy of Engineering, 2004, p. 21).

Despite these commitments to sustainable development, there is little evidence showing that most engineering students are learning about it. Although engineering students nowadays seem to show more awareness of environmental issues, they lack knowledge of definitions of and approaches to

- sustainable development
- key sustainable development principles and concepts such as the precautionary principle and inter- and intra-generational equity

- social justice in general
- and how to deal with stakeholder participation in sustainable development (Azapagic et al., 1999).

In a recent workshop on engineering design and sustainability, education researchers confirmed that students see the application of tools for sustainability, such as Life-Cycle Assessment (LCA), and the practice of engineering as contradictory:

> They [students] expressed that the particular focus on LCA would mean that 'functionality is made secondary' or that they would have to 'only think of the environment', which students expressed as a puzzle or contradiction to their understanding of engineering. The LCA is perceived as a borderline engineering related task. The researchers did not see much evidence that environmental issues are perceived as a required component of what makes a product 'functional'. A different version of the same argument surfaces, when students express LCAs are more valuable for end-users and less valuable for engineers (Strobel et al., 2009, p. 11).

This book cannot address all of these knowledge gaps; but it hopes to provide plausible answers as to why these gaps exist. We will analyze how traditional engineering design courses might be contributing to these knowledge gaps in the next chapter.

References

ASEE Board of Directors. (1999). "ASEE Statement on Sustainable Development Education." http://www.asee.org/about/Sustainable_Development.cfm

Ausubel, J. H., and H. Sladovich. (1989). Technology and Environment. Washington, DC: NAE.

Azapagic, A., S. Perdan, and D. Shallcross. (1999). "How much do engineering students know about sustainable development? The findings of an international survey and possible implications for the engineering curriculum." *European Journal of Engineering Education, 30*(1): 1–19.

Fiksel, J. (2006). "Sustainability and resilience: toward a systems approach." *Sustainability: Science, Practice and Policy* 2(2). (open access journal at http://ejournal.nbii.org/archives/vol2iss2/0608—028.fiksel.pdf.)

Hughes, A. C., and T. P. Hughes, Eds. (2000). *Systems, experts, and computers: the systems approach in management and engineering, World War II and after.* Dibner Institute Studies in the History of Science and Technology. Cambridge: MIT Press.

IEEE. (1991). Preparing for a Sustainable Society. Proceedings of the 1991 International Symposium on Technology and Society.

Lucena, J. (2003). "Flexible Engineers: History, challenges, and opportunities for engineering education." *Bulletin of Science, Technology, and Society, 23*(6): 419–435.

National Academy of Engineering. (2004). *The Engineer of 2020: Visions of Engineering in the New Century.* Washington, DC: The National Academies Press.

Neumayer, E. (1999).*Weak versus strong sustainability exploring the limits of two opposing paradigms.* Cheltenham, UK: E. Elgar.

Prendergast, J. (1993). Engineering sustainable development. *Civil Engineering, 63*(10): 39–42.

Strobel, J., I. Hua, F. Jun, and C. Harris. (2009). *Students' attitudes and threshold concepts towards engineering as an environmental career: Research by participatory design of an educational game.*

"Sustaining Sustainable Design," Mudd Design Workshop VII, Claremont, CA.

Velazquez, L. E., N. E. Munguia, and M. A. Romo. (1999). Education for sustainable development: the engineer of the 21st century. *European Journal of Engineering Education* 24(4): 359–370.

World Federation of Engineering Organizations. (1997). "Commitment to sustainable development. Resolution adopted by the WFEO General Assembly."

Zwally, K. D. (1996). *Highlights of the recommendations of the President's Council on Sustainable Development.* Energy Conversion Engineering Conference (IECEC), Washington DC: IECEC.

Strategy: Listening for and Making Objections (Refuting)

Lecturers and speakers participating in discussions often need to object to or argue against something someone has presented or proposed. Although any topic can be refuted, in academic discussions, several factors seem to be met with objections more than others. For example, people often question speakers about the cost of something, how well a solution works, or the reliability of the data. Some topics to prepare objections to or prepare to defend are listed.

Topic	Sample Objection
Financial	That seems expensive. Is it affordable?
Time Constraints	I'm not sure we have the time to examine that in depth. How long will it take?
Reliability	Are the results accurate? Will that be an effective solution?
Complexity	That method seems really complicated. Is it practical?
Advantages versus Disadvantages	Are there more pros than cons? The drawbacks seem to outnumber the benefits. Is it worth it?
Materials or Components	Are those the strongest materials? I'm not sure those parts will measure what we need them to measure.

Some general language can be used to make objections as well.

However,

But, what about . . . ?

No, I don't think so.

I don't know about that.

That's not a good idea because . . . .

That's debatable.

I'm not so sure about that.

Practice Activity: Making Objections

Read these sentences from the reading. Write an objection to each statement. The first one has several objections included for you as examples. Note that this is an activity to practice the language and it doesn't matter if your answer is factually correct.

1. Due to its reliance on technological solutions, most engineers have traditionally supported this approach.

   Is this always the best approach? Can we afford these technological solutions?

   _____

2. This view argues for the protection of natural resources even at the cost of development opportunities—and an example of that is saving the spotted owl even if it means losing growth opportunities for the timber industry.

   _____

   _____

3. A lot of people think that engineering programs today aren't spending enough time on sustainability.

   _____

   _____

4. This systems approach to sustainability has become institutionalized in a small number of engineering education programs such as University of Michigan's Engineering Sustainable Systems dual-degree.

   _____

   _____

Practice Activity: Overcoming Objections

Identify sentences from the reading in which the writer seems to be addressing an objection or concern. One has been listed for you.

1. Although sustainable development did not challenge engineers to compete in the international arena in the same way that economic competitiveness has done since the 1990s, it became a problem for some engineers to solve through a systems approach.

2. _____

_____

_____

_____

3. _____

_____

_____

_____

4. _____

_____

_____

_____

Speaking

Managing a Q & A Session

At some point in your academic or professional career, you will have to answer questions about your research or ideas. Many people find this stressful, but there are some strategies and words and phrases you can use to best manage these situations.

Prepare in advance. Predict questions your listeners might ask you about the content and prepare answers for those questions.

Repeat the question before you answer. Repeating helps others in the audience hear what was asked and gives you the opportunity to paraphrase to make sure you understood the question.

Be concise. Keep your answers short and make sure to answer only the question the listener asked.

Hesitate. Don't be afraid to use hesitations to give yourself a few seconds to think. Common hesitations include words and phrases such as *well, okay,* or *let me think*, or verbal sounds such as *umm* or *hmm*.

Don't be afraid to admit you don't know an answer. Tell a listener that you're not sure or that you'd like to research more information. Suggest meeting after the session or exchanging contact information. It's better to say you don't know an answer than to give incorrect information.

Ask people to speak louder, slower, or use different words if necessary for you to understand the question. Phrase your question in such a way that the person knows what you want. For example, don't just ask the person to repeat a question; ask the person to say it louder because you could not hear it.

Practice Activity: Discussing Q & A

Answer these questions with a partner.

1. Have you ever participated in a Q & A session? What was your role (asking questions or answering questions)? Was it a positive or negative experience?

2. What makes Q & A challenging as both a listener and a speaker?

3. Have you used any of the tips listed in the box? Do you have any other suggestions to share with the other groups?

Listening 2: Managing a Q & A Session

Listening to a Discussion (video)

Q & A sessions are common in academic settings. Listen to a student answering questions after he gives a presentation. Discuss these questions in a small group.

Focus on Language

1. What types of things did the audience member question or object to? (<u>Note</u>: Don't worry about writing exact words.)

_____

_____

2. What questions or words did the audience member use when making objections? (<u>Note</u>: Don't worry about writing exact words.)

_____

_____

3. Did the speaker use any hesitations? Which ones?

_____

_____

4. What strategies did the speaker use to manage the Q & A session? Do you think these were adequate? Would you recommend others?

_____

_____

5. Write any phrases or idioms you are not familiar with. Discuss what they mean and in which type of interaction they are appropriate.

_____

_____

Focus on Tone

1. How certain is the speaker of the answers? Is the speaker more confident in some answers than others? How do you know?

   _____

   _____

2. What is the attitude of the audience member asking the questions? How can you tell?

   _____

   _____

3. What messages or emotions are conveyed in tone? Describe the situation.

   _____

   _____

Focus on Nonverbal Communication

1. What nonverbal cues are used to show how the audience members feel? Are any of these inappropriate? Why or why not?

   _____

   _____

2. Who has the most expressive facial expressions and gestures? Do these positively or negatively affect the interaction?

   _____

   _____

3. Do the nonverbal cues match the tone and word choice?

_____

_____

4. Has this student answered questions in a Q & A before? What nonverbal cues support your opinion?

_____

_____

Summary

1. In your opinion, how does the speaker manage the Q & A session? What would you recommend the speaker do again? What would you recommend the speaker change for future sessions?

_____

_____

2. If the audience members asking the questions had a chance to improve this interaction, what changes would you recommend to her?

_____

_____

3. Were both the speaker and the audience member asking questions satisfied with the outcome of this Q & A session? What verbal and nonverbal cues support your opinion?

_____

_____

4. Would you want the audience member asking questions in your audience? Why or why not?

_____

_____

Part 3: Engineering Innovation

Getting Started

Part 1 discussed problem solving and presenting research. Innovation is important in any field and there are a myriad of inventions in the different fields of engineering. For example, electrical engineers may create hardware or circuit boards (i.e. for computers), while civil engineers create plans for bridges, highways, or buildings. Answer these questions with a partner.

1. What are some inventions that are important to the 21st century? What were some inventions important in the 20th century? Why did these make your list?

2. Is innovation important in every field? Describe how it is important in the field of study you are interested in pursuing. Can you think of any fields where it is not important?

Strategy: Listening for Ideal Breaks for Interruptions

Lectures are often long; they can be 45, 50, 60, or 75 minutes or even longer. Depending on the class size, some lecturers in English-speaking universities are accustomed to and welcome interruptions from the students. It is a good idea to listen for ideal breaks and interrupt at the best time. Additionally, it is good to notice certain words or phrases that a speaker uses to let you know the answer to your question is over and he or she is getting back to the lecture (whether it be on the same topic from before your question or on a new topic). Some ideal times to interrupt are:

When the speaker mentions a figure or reference from the textbook

> Now, remember the figure from the textbook? The bullseye/sustainability model vs. the Mickey Mouse model? [Student might say: I do remember that model, but I'm not sure I understand how it relates to . . . .]

Before the speaker starts defining terms or begins a new topic.

> At this point, I want to review some of these key terms. [Student might say: Before you do that, can I ask a question?]

After definitions or another interruption

Ok, back to the story. [Student might say: I have a question before we continue the story if I could.]

After questions in which the speaker is asking for a response from the listeners

Well, let's see how much you know about topics related to sustainable development. This is a survey that was given to engineering students around 2000. Do you know all of these? [Student might say: I'm not familiar with these. Where can I read more about them?]

When announcing a new topic is about to begin

Moving on . . . .

Now let's turn to . . . .

When the speaker gives a nonverbal cue, such as taking a drink of water, erasing the board, pausing, or changing the visual

There are certain way to be polite when you interrupt:

Sorry, but . . .

Excuse me . . .

Can I ask a question?

Can I jump in here?

I have a question related to this.

I'd like to ask something here.

There are also certain ways to get back to the topic after the question has been addressed:

Anyway . . .

As I was saying . . .

Now, moving forward . . .

Practice Activity: Interrupting and Getting Back to the Topic

Form a group of three. Choose one paragraph from a textbook you are using for another class or an article you need to read for research. Take turns reading your "lecture" to the other members of your group. Manage their interruptions by answering questions and getting back to the topic. When it is your turn to interrupt, try to do so during appropriate breaks in the content. Then answer these questions.

1. Were there any appropriate breaks in the content to interrupt?

   _____

   _____

2. Could the speakers have done anything differently to allow for interruptions?

   _____

   _____

3. What words or phrases were used to interrupt? To get back to the topic?

   _____

   _____

4. Which words or phrases were most effective or sounded best?

   _____

   _____

5. Do you have any other words or phrases to add to the list?

   _____

   _____

Research Strategy: Creating an Outline

When preparing a presentation, it is a good idea to prepare an outline. Your outline should include the main topics, your key supporting points, and any details you want to tell the listeners.

Creating an outline in advance can help in several ways:

- It can help you organize into a coherent manner so the listeners will easily be able to follow your ideas.

- It can help you see when you have too much information and you can then delete the less important details.

- It can help you determine when some of your points are weak and then you can find more details to support those points.

Practice Activity: Creating an Outline

Choose a textbook chapter from one of the books in your other classes or one in your field of study. Imagine you are going to convert this chapter into a lecture. Prepare an outline of the main points (MP), key supporting ideas (KS), and details (D). Continue on a separate piece of paper if necessary.

Topic: _____

Introduction:_____

_____

_____

_____

MP: _____

KS: _____

D: _____

D: _____

D: _____

KS: _____

D: _____

D: _____

D: _____

KS: _____

D: _____

D: _____

D: _____

MP: _____

D: _____

D: _____

D: _____

KS: _____

D: _____

D: _____

D: _____

KS: _____

D: _____

D: _____

D: _____

Conclusions: _____

_____

_____

_____

Now imagine you learned your presentation will be twice as long as you have detailed. Add additional information to your outline.

Then imagine you learned that your time slot at the conference will be half as long as you originally planned for. Edit to delete any information you do not think should be included.

Vocabulary Power

There are a number of terms and phrases in this lecture that you may encounter in other academic settings. Add at least five vocabulary items to your vocabulary notebook or log.
Match the words or phrases in bold with the definition on the right.

_____ 1. Because of the variable and uncertain engineering properties of geologic materials, tunnel design requires an **iterative** procedure where initial design assumptions must be reevaluated based on observed field conditions throughout construction.

_____ 2. However, both analytical and numerical approaches need to be **validated** and analyzed in light of historical performance of tunnels during earthquakes.

_____ 3. Underground structures suffer **appreciably** less damage than surface structures.

_____ 4. Underground facilities constructed in soils can be expected to suffer more damage compared to openings constructed in **competent** rock.

_____ 5. Tunnels are more stable under a **symmetric** load.

_____ 6. Duration of strong-motion shaking during earthquakes is of **utmost** importance because it may cause fatigue failure and, therefore, large deformations.

_____ 7. These frequencies, which rapidly **attenuate** with distance, may be expected mainly at small distances from the causative fault.

_____ 8. The ground motion **parameters** are then evaluated.

a. diminish

b. authenticated, supported

c. supreme, paramount

d. rules or limits

e. balanced

f. noticeable, perceptible

g. repetitive

h. qualified, fit

Listening 3: Engineering Innovations: Tunnels

Listening to a Lecture

As you listen, try to write the main points, key supporting ideas, and details in an outline form.

Checking Your Understanding: Main Ideas

Review your notes. Listen again to the lecture if necessary. Decide whether each statement is true (T) or false (F) based on the lecture.

_____ Society as a whole becoming less dependent on tunnels has lessened the concerns over the consequences of failure.

_____ Tunnel design is a big challenge for engineers.

_____ Designing earthquake-resistant tunnels is less advanced than designing other surface earthquake-resistant structures.

_____ Underground structures, like tunnels, have suffered less structural damage during earthquakes than above-ground structures.

_____ The design of tunnels in non-seismic regions requires three main steps.

Group Presentation

Tunnels have been built around the world and for a variety of reasons. Some are used for vehicular traffic, others are used to supply water, and still others are used for utilities, such as electrical power. Some tunnels are simple passageways for people to move between buildings or across roads or to help wildlife avoid the dangers of manmade roads. Other tunnels have been built for military purposes. As you know from the lecture, construction types vary depending on the geology and/or purpose of the tunnel. Historically, tunnels have existed for thousands of years. Some famous tunnels include the Thirlmere Aqueduct in England, which is the world's longest tunnel, and the Moffat Tunnel in Colorado, which is the highest railroad tunnel in the United States.

In teams of three, do some light research on tunnels and choose one tunnel to research in more depth. Prepare a presentation, including visual aids, on the tunnel you choose. Prepare your presentation to be delivered to the rest of the class.

Name/location of tunnel: _____

Things to include: _____

_____

_____

_____

_____

Rapid Vocabulary Review

From the three answers on the right, circle the one that best explains the vocabulary item on the left as it is used in this unit.

Vocabulary	Answers		
Synonyms			
innovation	creation	replication	fantasy
immersed	distracted	interested	covered
implementation	executed	conclusion	consideration
concise	brief	intelligent	unhappy
amplified	increased	stabilized	lessened
incidence	timing	occurrence	effect
dominant	neglible	outstanding	paramount
luster	brilliance	flash	obscurity
materialize	continue	appear	exist
strive	take by force	quit suddenly	work hard
Combinations and Associations			
code of _____	principles	rules	ethics
associated _____	on	in	with
comply _____	with	upon	for
real- _____	world	vision	fact
_____ out of	started	grew	initiated
based _____	in	of	on
pop _____	up	about	under
literature _____	study	documents	review
_____ lines	safety	end	life
given _____	them	that	then

⇨✗⇦ Synthesizing: Projects and Presentations

Short In-Class Assignments	Longer Outside Assignments
Q & A	Reaching the World's Oil Supply
Form groups of three. Take turns telling your teammates about something you are studying in another course. They will ask questions when you are finished. Do what you can to answer their questions. Make sure to be an active listener when they present and ask questions after their presentations.	Review the concept of sustainability discussed in Part 2. Do some light research on the state of the world's oil supply and which countries are producing it, where other reserves might exist, and if alternative solutions are needed. Prepare a presentation on your findings. Be prepared for other students to interrupt as you present your findings.
Be Compelling and Sell It	Your Own Three-Minute Thesis
Pull a random item from your backpack or totebag . . . any item that you brought to class. Write a 30-second "commercial" trying to sell the item to your classmates. Practice your commercial with a small group before presenting it to the whole class.	Prepare a three-minute thesis on a topic you are studying. Follow the rules of the competition and consider the criteria with which presentations are evaluated as you prepare yours. Prepare to deliver your thesis to the judges (your classmates) on your assigned day. Remember that they will be evaluating you using the criteria.

Vocabulary Log

To increase your vocabulary knowledge, write a definition or translation for each vocabulary item. Then write an original phrase, sentence, or note that will help you remember the vocabulary item.

Vocabulary Item	Definition or Translation	Your Original Phrase, Sentence, or Note
1. marginally		
2. lacking		
3. qualitative		
4. facilitation		
5. interdisciplinary		
6. appropriated		
7. caveat		
8. accreditation		
9. rigorous		
10. component		
11. enrich		
12. symposium		
13. preoccupation		

Vocabulary Item	Definition or Translation	Your Original Phrase, Sentence, or Note
14. conception		
15. intrusive		
16. trend (n.)		
17. exemplify		
18. feasible		
19. confinement		
20. state-of-the-practice		
21. cross-sectional		
22. fabricate		
23. gadget		
24. on the market		
25. compact (adj.)		

Appendix 1: Review of Note-Taking Formats

As you are taking notes, you will need to practice certain conventions to keep up with the lecture. Even if you can go back to a professor's PowerPoint or hand-outs, you can't write every word. Here are some good note-taking strategies that you may already be using in English or in your own language:

- **Be brief.** Write only the major points and important information and don't be concerned with spelling and grammar. What would you need to write to remember this idea from the lecture?

  The professor says:

  > *He suggested that rules that govern the possible utterances in human language are well-defined in every language.*

  You could write:

  > Rules well-defined — all human lnges.

- **Use abbreviations in your notes.**

  w/ = with
  w/o = without
  w/in = within
  dif't = different
  impt = important

- **Use symbols.**

  → leads to or results in
  ← comes from
  + with
  – without

- **Other good practices are:**

  —Drop the last several letters of a word. For example, substitute *appropriate* with *approp.* or *cont.* for *continue*.

  —Drop some of the internal vowels of a word. For example, *lrg.* for *large* or *lnge.* for *language*.

  —Mark main ideas with a star (*).

  —Underline <u>important</u> ideas.

Flow Chart

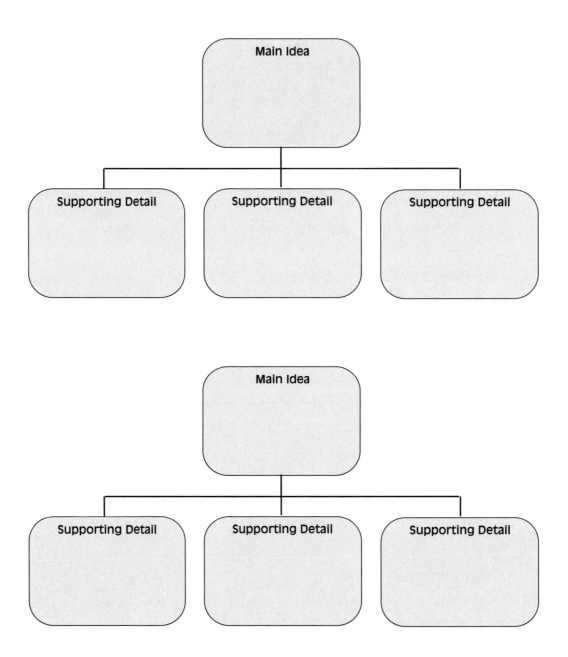

Mind Maps

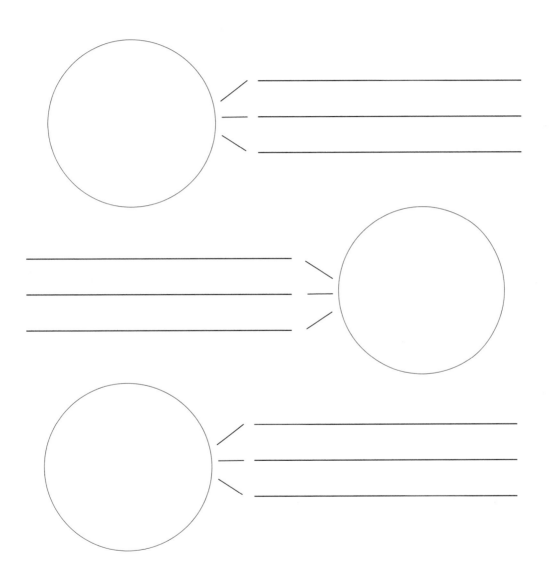

Some Sample Notes from Unit 2 Lecture

◯	
2004 brought	2004 tsunami—Indian Ocean
tsm. public	11 countries, over 200,000 dead
attention	
	Means harbor wave—Japanese
Meaning of	tidal wave misnomer (wrong name)
'Tsunami'	Seismic wave misleading—not always earthquake
◯	
◯	

Appendix 2: Debate (Oral Arguments) Guidelines

In preparation for the debate, conduct research on the topic. Write three reasons to support the topic and three reasons not to support it. You need to consider both sides of the argument so that you can argue compellingly with the other team.

Pro 1: _____

Pro 2: _____

Pro 3: _____

Con 1: _____

Con 2: _____

Con 3: _____

Preparing as a Team

Now work with your team. Take turns discussing your pros and cons. Select the strongest arguments, particularly those that can be supported by research. Select arguments that you think will be difficult for the other team to refute. Also think about responses you could use to counter the other team's arguments.

Arguments:

_____

_____

_____

Counterarguments:

_____

_____

_____

Debate Format:

> Pro team member gives an introductory statement on the topic to present/preview pro opinion
>
> Con team gives an introductory statement on the topic to present/preview con opinion
>
> Con team member presents the first argument
>
> Pro team rebuts with counterargument.
>
> Pro team member presents the next argument.
>
> Con team rebuts with counterargument.
>
> Team members will continue exchanging arguments and rebuttals until all team members have presented their arguments and counterarguments.
>
> Open discussion (15 minutes)
>
> Pro team member gives closing statement/summary on pro team's argument.
>
> Con team member gives closing statement/summary on con team's argument.

Team member giving introductory statement _____

Team member giving closing statement _____

Other arguments:

_____

_____

_____

_____

_____